The Intern I... W9-CHS-330

The Guidebook for Finding and Landing Great Internships

KAREN

RENEÉ

Intern Bridge, Inc.
with content by Laura Szadvari

First Printing

Intern Bridge, Inc.

The Intern Insider:
The Guidebook for Finding and Landing Great Internships

Intern Bridge, Inc. with content by Laura Szadvari

© Copyright 2009 by Intern Bridge, Inc.
All Rights Reserved

ISBN 978-0-9799373-6-1

First Printing January 2009

This publication is designed to provide accurate and authoritative information in regard to the subject matter covered. It is sold with the understanding that neither the author nor the publisher is engaged in rendering legal, accounting, or other professional service. If legal advice or other expert assistance is required, the services of a competent professional should be sought.

Further, although every precaution has been taken in the preparation of this book, the author and publisher assume no responsibility for errors or omissions. Nor is any liability assumed for damages resulting from the use of the information contained herein.

Published by Intern Bridge, Inc.
19 Railroad Street, Suite 3B
Acton, MA 01720

For sales information, please email Sales@InternBridge.com or call us at 800-531-6091.

Cover design/layout/production: bookpackgraphics@yahoo.com (Dan Berger)

Printed in U.S.A.

TABLE OF CONTENTS

SECTION ONE:
INTERNSHIP INFORMATION YOU NEED TO KNOW

SECTION TWO:
INSIDER INTERNSHIP LISTINGS

WHAT IS AN INTERNSHIP?

Internships are short-term, on-the-job learning experiences designed to allow you to apply knowledge gained in the classroom to a real-world, professional work setting. These work experiences may be paid or unpaid, for credit or not for credit, or full-time or part-time. Typically, you will complete an internship in a field related to your major, but this is not always the case. While summer internships tend to be the most popular, fall and spring internship opportunities are plentiful and, often, easier to obtain. The role that you would assume within the organization is often one with a fair amount of responsibility, especially if you are an upper-classman. Usually, there is also an educational component to the experience via assigned papers, projects, or readings from a faculty advisor. As both an employee and a student, you would learn through observation, participation, and reflection of what occurred during both the work experience and the academic experience.

WHY DO AN INTERNSHIP?

There are several reasons why you might consider doing an internship.

1. To test out a field of interest

Internships are a wonderful way to explore a field, industry, or profession you do not have a lot of (or any!) experience in. For example, a student who is thinking of becoming a doctor may want to do an internship at a hospital or in a doctor's office early in his or her college years. The pre-medical curriculum can be very challenging and difficult, so it might make sense, early on, to see if this is a viable career option for you. Alternatively, perhaps you are majoring in business, but thinking about going to law school. It would be a smart idea to see what the field of law is really like before you make the commitment (in time, energy, and money) to go to graduate school for three (very long) years.

2. To confirm a career choice

Similar to the reason above, it would make sense to obtain an internship in your proposed job field before you make the plunge into a full-time, permanent position. Looking ahead to post-graduation, you will want to remain with your first employer for no less than a year, preferably longer. In order to ensure that your first role out of college is a good fit for your skills, interests, and abilities, you might consider doing a "trial run" for a semester or two in the job you *think* you would like to have after college. Often times, the work is very different from what you thought it would be, and you may come to realize that you are much better suited to a different occupation.

3. To gain professional work experience

Like most college students, the extent of your work experience is probably in the retail, food and beverage, child care, and/or outdoor maintenance fields. This is fine! You have no doubt learned some very valuable lessons and honed some extremely marketable skills by working these jobs. However, as you move through your four years of college, future employers are going to want to see more professional types of work experiences. They do not necessarily have to be paid positions and they can certainly be short-term opportunities. The specific work you do can be related to your major, or not, but the role you play in the organization should be indicative of the skills and abilities you can bring to the table post-graduation. In a competitive, tight job market, these experiences will make you stand out from the crowd and, quite frankly, the more you have of them, the better prepared and qualified a candidate you will be. Internships meet the criteria that employers are looking for and, therefore, you should do as many as possible to allow yourself to grow and develop as a future business professional.

4. To make contacts in the field

Any career counselor will tell you that networking is the single most important thing you can do to effectively increase your opportunities for obtaining the best jobs available. While the percentages differ according to the source, it is commonly agreed upon that most jobs are found through word of mouth. You have most likely heard the saying, "it's not what you know, it's *who* you know," and while that is not *always* the case, it is true more often than you might think. To this end, it makes excellent business sense to start making as many professional contacts as you can, as early in your college years as you can. While it would be ideal to develop a large base of professional contacts within your specific field of interest, it is perfectly fine to acquire a broader contact base as well. Why? Simple – the more people you know, the more people they know. Think about the social media site, Facebook. All of your friends have friends… and all of those friends have friends…and so on and so forth. It works the same way in the professional work arena. Doing an internship will expose you to numerous people in the workplace and some of them will most likely be very influential. Do a good job for them and, undoubtedly, they will do what they can to help you get to where you want to be.

5. To get credit

Many schools offer the opportunity to obtain academic credit for an internship experience. Depending on the specific requirements of the program, sometimes this credit can be applied towards your major. Other times, the credit may count as elective credits. You will have to check with the appropriate office at your own school, but it is definitely worth investigating, especially if you need extra credits to graduate. Please keep in mind that there may be additional fees charged for internship credit, and that internships done for credit over a summer session may incur extra tuition charges. Your advisor can assist you with determining what makes sense for your own unique situation.

6. To round out your resume

Future employers will evaluate your candidacy for open positions depending, in part, on what you display on your resume. You will want to make sure you have created a document that is very well-rounded and portrays a successful balance of academic achievement, extracurricular involvement, and professional work experience. If you are lacking in this last area, you will want to consider bolstering that category with an internship or two. Resumes that are disproportionately heavy in one area and light in another are potential red flags to employers who are looking for great, all-around, well-balanced candidates.

WHAT ARE SOME OF THE THINGS I NEED TO THINK ABOUT BEFORE DOING AN INTERNSHIP?

Doing an internship is a great idea. Doing two or more internships is even better. However, there are several things you will want to consider before jumping outright into an internship experience. Just a little bit of careful planning on your part will ensure that your experience is the most valuable it can be.

Things to consider:

• **Your interests:**
Ask yourself the following questions – What are you interested in? What would you like to explore? What have you always wanted to try? Write the answers to these questions down and then try to narrow the field according to your top choices and the opportunities available. Remember, you can certainly do multiple internships, so keep your mind open to all potential options. Never pass up a good opportunity waiting for the "perfect" one to come around. Like full-time jobs, there are pros and cons to every position, and it is often a matter of picking the best, if not ideal, internship available.

• **Credit versus Non-Credit:**
Depending on the program(s) available at your school, it may be possible to obtain academic credit for an internship experience. At some schools, and with certain internship sites, it is mandatory. Sometimes obtaining credit

involves additional fees and/or tuition. Most of the time, it involves additional coursework and maybe even an extra class. At some schools, it is not possible to obtain course credit *and* get paid for the work you are doing at the internship site. You will need to assess whether or not it makes sense to try to get credit for your internship and proceed forward with what is best for your specific situation. Keep in mind, however, that as a general rule, future employers don't much care whether or not your internships are for credit. They are simply looking for the experience you gained as a result of them.

• **Goals and Learning Objectives:**
Once you determine the field in which you would like to intern, it is important to further analyze what you hope to gain as a result of the internship experience itself. Are there certain skills and abilities you wish to develop or hone? Is there a particular talent or expertise you would like to improve? What do you wish to learn, study, or practice? Your advisor can help you create a structured learning plan, with specific goals and objectives, to make certain that you obtain the best work and academic experience possible.

• **Logistics:**
Before you commit to a particular internship position, you should think about the logistics involved in successfully completing it. Think about where the internship is located – will you have a long commute? Will transportation be an issue? What about the hours required? Will you be able to work the internship into your course schedule? It's usually best to arrange your schedule so that you have "chunks" of time (3 hours or more) to work. This allows you to focus, in-depth, on a task or project at any given time. Employers are typically very flexible when it comes to working around a student's class schedule, but there may be certain times when it is necessary to be in the office. Think about setting up your classes on Mondays, Wednesdays, and Fridays, or, alternatively, on Tuesdays and Thursdays. Having two or three full days per week to commit to an internship usually results in an excellent, comprehensive experience. Determine whether or not there are required training classes or certain pre-requisite courses that are necessary before you start the internship. Are you willing to do the required work ahead of time, or does it make more sense to find another opportunity? The point here is that you need to look beyond the big picture and consider the details involved in obtaining and completing any internship experience in which you are interested.

ARE THERE CERTAIN INTERNSHIP "FACTS" THAT I NEED TO KNOW?

There are certain universal facts about internships that would be useful for you to know as you begin to explore different opportunities.

• Most internships are unpaid. Sad, but true. However, "most" does not mean all. You will find that certain fields more easily allow for paid internships, most notably computer science, engineering, and business. Sometimes, non-profit organizations (who typically cannot afford to pay their interns) will receive grants that allow them to compensate their interns. Other times, companies will provide interns with perks that are not necessarily tied to a paycheck, such as gas or gift cards, concert tickets, conference attendance, or tuition and book assistance. You may have noticed that "money" was not a listed reason as to why you might want to pursue an internship. If you need money, you are better off seeking a part-time job. If you want professional experience, you should look for an internship. If you would like to (or need to) combine both options, consider doing a part-time internship concurrently with a part-time job.

• When students think about internships, they usually think about them for the summer. But, while the majority of companies who offer internships offer them during the summer months (and tend to pay their interns more often during this time as well), there are plenty of opportunities to be found during the fall and spring. While the fall and spring internships are usually just as valuable as the summer ones, the bonus for students is that these internships tend to be a bit less competitive. Why? Because students sometimes have so many other activities going on during the school year that they can not accommodate yet another commitment. As a result, if you are willing to arrange your life so that you can work an internship during the fall and/or spring semesters, you may find that you have many more options to choose from and far fewer students to compete against.

• Just because an organization does not advertise or post for an intern does not necessarily mean that it won't consider hiring one. Some organizations assume that if they can't afford to pay someone, no student would be interested. Other companies have never hosted an intern before and have no idea how to incorporate such a program into their structure. Still other organizations may not feel that they have enough work, or enough work of the right caliber, to justify hiring an intern. Therefore, even if the company does not seem to be actively recruiting for interns, it never hurts to approach a company of interest and inquire as to whether or not they would consider hiring you, especially if you are willing to work for free. The worst that can happen is that they say no. Nothing gained, nothing lost, but at least it's worth a shot.

• Internships can often lead to full-time job opportunities. Many companies, especially the larger ones, hire interns in order to build their full-time recruiting pipeline as early as possible. This means that a company may hire you for the summer with the expectation that you will do well and consider coming back the following year, after you graduate. This is not only a smart recruiting strategy for the firm, but also a wonderful opportunity for you, as a student, to do a "test run" at the company. While you are never guaranteed a full-time, permanent position, you may be able to secure an offer by the end of your internship if you do a good job and if the opportunity exists. If an opportunity does not exist at that particular company, you still may be able to obtain a permanent position (or at least some leads toward finding one) by asking for contacts at and referrals to other companies in the same industry. Assuming you do well in your internship, most employers would be more than happy to help you find a full-time job by recommending you to their contacts at other places within your field of interest.

• It is critically important to be aware of internship application deadlines. Some organizations, especially those agencies within the federal government, can have application deadlines as early as *one year* in advance of when the internship would start. This means that you would potentially need to apply for a summer internship with the government as early as the summer before! Larger companies who hire numerous interns into a more structured, organized internship program tend to do their summer intern recruiting during the fall and spring semesters prior. Smaller organizations may have deadlines only a month or so out from when the internship would begin. Still others may not have any set deadline and perform their intern hiring on a case-by-case basis. Too many well-qualified students have missed out on the opportunity to obtain their internship of choice because they have missed the deadline to apply. Do not let this happen to you. Plan early and wisely so that you may take advantage of each and every internship opportunity that comes your way.

WHERE ARE INTERNSHIP OPPORTUNITIES FOUND?

Internship opportunities exist in all different sorts of organizations and industries. As you start to explore different options, you may find that some of these opportunities are with very small, local companies and others are with larger, national companies. You may even come across some that are in different states or countries from where you are located. There are pros and cons associated with each individual internship experience, so it is very important to keep your mind open to all possibilities. Try to keep a spreadsheet or a list noting the strengths and weaknesses of each internship opportunity as you come across it, and remember that no single internship experience will ever be perfect. Below are some general guidelines that may help you in weighing your choices.

Local internships:

These internships may be easier to get by virtue of the fact that they are in smaller, less structured companies. If your school is located in a small town, it is likely that your school may already have an established relationship with a company, or that a particular company has hosted interns from the school in the past. Sometimes this makes it easier for you to get hired during the fall or spring semesters. There is also typically less competition for internships in smaller companies, which is quite silly because the opportunities to gain professional business experience can be just as good, if not better, at smaller companies than at larger ones. Quite often, you will find that you have to perform many different roles in a smaller company, which can result in gaining very broad business exposure over an entire array of tasks. Smaller, local companies may also be able to offer you more flexibility in terms of the assignments and projects you work on. They may be better able to shape the internship around your goals and objectives as a student, and allow you the chance to create your own position. So, while these types of internships may not carry the same "brand name" appeal as the larger, more commonly recognized firms, they can still be very valuable in terms of the experience and exposure they provide.

Regional internships:

Regional internships may be with larger, more structured and established firms, who often hire numerous interns from the surrounding areas and bring them all together into one single regional office in cities like New York, Washington DC, Atlanta, Dallas, Chicago, Minneapolis, Seattle, San Francisco, or Los Angeles. Many times, these internship programs are rotational in nature, which means that, as a student, you spend the semester or summer moving around within many different areas of that company's business. As a result, you come away with a broad knowledge base relative to the workings of that particular organization. Other times, the company may be so large that you get placed in one particular division of the business and develop an expertise in that specific area. Because these internship programs tend to be larger in scope, it is more likely that you will get paid and/or obtain the opportunity to experience some corporate "perks" of the job (concerts, tours, outings, etc.). While these companies and programs may be well-recognized and well-established in nature, the application and selection process may be more competitive. The atmosphere and culture may be less personal than that of a smaller firm and, while some companies do provide housing and transportation assistance, you may find that the logistics involved in such an internship opportunity are somewhat cumbersome and difficult to manage.

Out-of-State internships:

Sometimes, internship opportunities in certain fields will be quite limited and will only be available in certain locations during certain times of the year. As a student, you will need to make the choice as to whether or not it is worth it to you to pursue these opportunities. It may require taking a leave of absence from school to travel to where the internship is located. It may necessitate taking out an additional loan or working two or more part-time jobs in order to finance the internship opportunity. It may even mean postponing your graduation date and/or graduate school so that you can take advantage of the experience offered to you. While these types of opportunities may be somewhat challenging to fit in to your schedule, they are often the kinds of experiences that are extremely valuable to your long term success in your field of choice. For example, these types of internships are in fields like theatre and acting, music and film production, fashion design, biomedical research, veterinary science, political science, and anthropology/archeology. While it is unfair to say that you would not be able to find similar opportunities in your own home state, it is unrealistic to think that you would have an easy time doing so. There may come a point where you will want to consider doing an out-of-state internship and, in that case, you would be wise to seek guidance and advice from both your parents and your school advisors.

International internships:

International internships are available during both the fall and spring semesters, as well as during the summer. There are several companies that assist students looking for international experience in different fields. Many of these organizations will actually match students up with the specific internship opportunities that fit their interests. Unfortunately, most of these places charge a pretty hefty fee for their services, but for students looking for unique or unusual internship experiences, the money may very well be worth it. It is always advisable to perform due diligence on these types of organizations before you choose to work with one – read their brochures cover to cover, ask for references, talk to previous students, obtain guidance from your career services office, and ask your parents for their input. While the majority of these organizations are completely legitimate, there will always be some that are better organized and more professionally managed than others. An alternative to this type of international internship is obtaining an internship through an approved study abroad program at your university. Many of the fall and spring international exchange or study abroad programs have experiential work components where you can gain professional work experience in a particular business setting. For students whose schools award academic credit for internship experiences, it may be necessary to get "pre-approval" before you leave the country. Work with your academic services department, study abroad office, or career services office to check on your school's particular requirements.

DO I HAVE TO FULFILL ANY REQUIREMENTS BEFORE I COMMIT TO AN INTERNSHIP?

Different schools will have different requirements for students wishing to complete an internship. It is best to check with your advisor regarding these rules and regulations. In general, you may need to think about the following factors before you commit to working in an internship position.

1. Your GPA:

At many schools, students need to carry a minimum GPA in order to be allowed to complete an internship. This rule makes very good sense from an academic perspective. If you are not doing well enough in your coursework to maintain the minimum GPA that your school requires, you really have no business spending time away from your studies!

2. The number of credits you have completed:

Most schools will also dictate that students need to have completed a minimum number of credits before pursuing any type of internship experience (sometimes within the major, sometimes overall). This makes academic sense, as well. The more coursework you have under your belt by the time the internship begins, the more likely you are to be able to make successful and effective contributions to the company at which you intern. This policy also makes economic sense from the perspective of the employer. While employers understand that you are still learning and developing as a young business professional, at the same time, they expect that you will have at least a basic academic foundation from which you can grow. They expect to have to train you in some, if not most areas - but they would prefer not to have to start at ground zero!

3. Obtaining a faculty sponsor and/or developing a learning plan:

In order to obtain academic credit at some schools, you will need to obtain the guidance and sponsorship of a faculty member in the academic department most relevant to the internship you are completing. Some schools will require that you develop a learning plan prior to commencing the internship and complete it during the semester in which you work. At some schools, you must also take a special internship class or seminar concurrently with your internship. Be sure to check with your advisor or academic services office for the specific rules at your school.

4. Specific departmental requirements:

Certain academic departments may have specific requirements for their students who are interested in pursuing an internship. In some instances, students may be allowed to intern only with pre-approved agencies (or go through a designated approval process prior to starting with a new site). In other situations, the academic department may determine that only students who have taken certain course pre-requisites may be allowed to intern. Sometimes these particular academic departments decide how much and in what ways credit can be awarded. The rules and regulations will vary from school to school and, often times, from department to department. Be sure you understand the processes and procedures in place before you accept any internship position.

HOW DO I GO ABOUT SEARCHING FOR AN INTERNSHIP?

Similar to a full-time job search, the internship search can be time-consuming and, at times, frustrating. However, the good news is that there are lots of different ways to go about your search. If you put in the required amount of time and understand, up front, that the search will take up a fair amount of your energy, you will undoubtedly succeed in securing an awesome opportunity. To make the search process as easy as possible, let's break down the available tools and resources into three distinct categories. Please note, however, that not all schools will have available all resources. Alternatively, other schools may have more resources at your disposal than you know what to do with. Therefore, you may have to wisely pick and choose how you spend your time.

1. Career Center Resources:

The very first stop that you should make on the road to internship success is at your school's career center (if your school has one). This is the office that typically houses internship listings and opportunities, sometimes broken out by major or field of interest. You may be so lucky as to find local, regional, national, and (possibly) international postings all in one place. Some schools will separate their internship listings by semester or will, at least, separate the summer opportunities from the academic year opportunities. Many schools will keep lists of where past interns worked so you can look through the companies and contact then directly if you see one that you like. The fact that they have hosted an intern from your school in the past makes it likely that they might consider hosting one again, if they have the need. Other schools will ask students to evaluate their internship experiences at the end of the term and will keep these evaluations in a binder so that other students can review them before accepting an internship offer. Many companies produce brochures, flyers, and other types of marketing pamphlets aimed at attracting interns from certain schools. Chances are that your career center has these materials available for you to peruse at your convenience and, if so, it would definitely behoove you to check them out. Finally, if your school is one that sponsors career fairs throughout the year, check and see if the career center has the old fair booklets from past years. Once again, you may see certain companies that, at least at one point, were interested in recruiting from your school. If you see particular companies that strike your interest, you should feel free to contact them to introduce yourself and state your desire to intern with them. While they may not have a current posting with your school, they may just decide to give you an opportunity if you can show that your interests, skills, and abilities mesh with their needs.

2. Internet Resources:

The internet is chock full of job search boards, many of them internship specific. Often, you can select your search criteria according to geographical preference, industry, role, and/or job function. There are literally hundreds of sites to choose from, but, like all things, some are better than others. You would be smart to check with your career center or academic services office to see if there are particular sites that they recommend. Alternatively, you can do a simple Google or Yahoo! search to try and find internship listings in your preferred area and field. The downside here is that you may have to weed through a lot of junk before you find what you are looking for.

3. Other Resources:

There are various other ways to find internship opportunities. Consider the following:

• Networking with family, friends, professors, advisors, past internship and employer managers, supervisors, and co-workers. Contact everyone you know and spread the word that you are looking for an internship. You never know what you might find.

• Tap into the alumni network at your school. Former students usually love to talk to current students and are typically more than happy to assist them with career-related issues. While these folks may not be able to actually offer you an internship position, chances are they might have some very helpful advice or be able to point you in the right direction/refer you to additional contact people. Also, see if your career center or alumni office maintains a list of career "mentors". These are specific people (alumni, friends of the university, current recruiters, etc.) who have volunteered to talk to students about a variety of issues related to both college and work. Because these individuals have willingly put their names on a list of potential people to be contacted, you should definitely feel free to take advantage of their generosity and solicit their advice. They may know of opportunities that you might be interested in.

• Check out the websites for professional organizations in the fields you are interested in. For example, if you are interested in journalism, look at the website for the Newspaper Association of America. If you are interested in history or historic preservation, go online to the American Association of Museums. Many of these sites will either post job and internship listings or direct you to other sites that do.

• Contact your local Chamber of Commerce and ask to have or borrow one of their directories. This type of informational guide usually lists the names, addresses, phone numbers, and contact people for different companies in the area and is usually organized according to industry. You can use the directory to generate a list of organizations that you might be interested in and then do further research on your own via their individual websites.

• Flip through your local Yellow Pages to find companies that you may be interested in targeting.

• Take a trip to your school or town library and ask the reference librarian to show you the section where they keep the local business directories and the books that list professional organizations in your area. You may find some good leads through this process.

Past students have said that the time spent looking for an internship is equivalent to the time spent on a semester-long class. While it may not take you quite that long, it is important to understand that finding an internship usually does not happen immediately, especially if you are looking for an experience in a competitive field, an uncommon field, a popular geographical location, or a very remote area. Start your search process early, and use every single resource available to you. Use both the "direct" way of finding an internship (applying to advertised postings) and the "indirect" way of finding an internship (conducting a targeted search by approaching companies you are interested in). If you put forth the appropriate amount of time, energy, and effort, you will undeniably be rewarded with an experience that is meaningful, enjoyable, and unquestionably successful.

HOW DO I APPLY FOR AN INTERNSHIP?

If you are applying to an internship that has been posted at your school or via a job board, you should follow the specific instructions given. You may be asked to mail or email a cover letter and resume, call for an appointment, or go to a website and apply online. Read the application guidelines carefully and do *exactly* as you are told. This is especially important if you are applying for a federal, state, or local government position, as these agencies sometimes have very detailed application procedures.

If you are conducting a more targeted search and find a company in which you are interested but do not see any open internship positions posted, it is advisable to do the following: Call the main telephone number listed for the company, introduce yourself as a student looking for an internship, and ask to speak to the person in charge of hiring interns. If the company is de-centralized, or if there is no one specific person in charge of internships, then ask to speak to the person in charge of the particular area of the business in which you are interested. Introduce yourself briefly to this individual, express your interest in the company, and ask if they would consider taking a look at your resume to see if there might be a need you could fill for them. They may be more inclined to consider you if you mention that you are not looking to get paid, but rather to get professional work experience in their particular industry. If you are uncomfortable making this type of a "cold" call, ask your parents, advisor, or career center counselor for some tips on making this easier. Rest assured, after you do this the first few times, it will get much easier! If you continue to feel ill at ease, you may certainly mail or email a cover letter and resume to the appropriate contact person (instead of calling), but please understand that, unfortunately, a letter or email is somewhat easier to ignore than a phone call. As a result, you might have more difficulty connecting with the person who could, ultimately, hire you as an intern.

Regardless of how you apply for an internship position, you will need to make sure that you have a well-crafted resume and an enthusiastic, engaging cover

17

letter prepared. Your school's career center should be able to help you create these documents, and you would be well advised to use their services. They are experts in this type of thing! Remember to personalize both your cover letter and resume for each and every internship position for which you apply.

While it certainly makes sense to have a really solid generic version of your resume at the ready in case you are asked, spur of the moment, to produce one, you should also attempt to create customized resumes, highlighting the relevant skills and abilities needed for each internship position. Tailoring your resume illustrates your attention to detail, your interest in the specific company and position, and your willingness to go the extra mile to get the job. This, alone, can often set you apart from the competition and give you a competitive edge, especially in those fields that are super popular or especially hard to break into.

Additionally, if your career center offers the opportunity to practice interviewing skills and techniques (often called "mock interviews"), definitely find the time to take advantage of this service. The more you practice, the better prepared you will be to interview effectively and comfortably, and the better chance you will have of landing a wonderful internship!

WHAT ARE EMPLOYERS LOOKING FOR IN AN INTERN?[1]

For the most part, the skills and abilities that employers seek in their interns are similar to those they seek in their full-time employees. Granted, as a college student, you do not have (nor are you expected to have) the same level of experience, expertise, or business acumen that more mature, seasoned workers have; however, you should be in (reasonable) possession of the most basic traits that any good, honest, hard-working employee would have.

Following, in no particular order, are some of the most important characteristics that employers want to see. Again, please understand that no one student will embody all of these qualities, but the more you have (and the better you can demonstrate them in your cover letter, resume, and interview), the more competitive a candidate you will be.

---

[1] Adapted from Loughborough University's Career Services homepage.

Problem-solving and analytical ability:
Can you dissect a problem and logically consider all solutions? Are you good at reasoning and thoroughly thinking through an issue before making a decision?

Computer/technical literacy:
Are you computer savvy? Is it easy for you to learn new software applications, and are you comfortable doing so?

Content knowledge:
Do you have a basic, foundational understanding of the field or industry in which you want to intern? Have you taken (at least) the relevant introductory courses in school?

Time-management, organization, and planning skills:
Can you effectively manage all of your responsibilities in an orderly, organized manner? Do you plan tasks and projects out in advance and break them into smaller pieces so that you are assured of a successful completion?

Research skills:
Are you good at finding, analyzing, and synthesizing information from different sources? Do you like to examine, explore, inspect and/or scrutinize?

The ability to multi-task:
Can you work on several different assignments at once without becoming overwhelmed? Can you manage yourself within a fast-paced, sometimes stressful environment?

A willingness to learn:
Are you open to learning more about the industry in which you are interning? Will you be willing to consider that it may not be what you expected?

Flexibility/adaptability:
Can you shift gears quickly, if needed? Can you adjust to changes in your duties and responsibilities? Will you be able to juggle competing priorities and rearrange them if necessary?

Dependability: Can you be counted on to fulfill your commitments to the organization? Will you show up on time on the days when you are expected? Will you be able to meet your deadlines?

The Intern Insider

Initiative:
Are you self-motivated? Will you volunteer to do more than what is asked of you? Will you seek out additional opportunities within the company if you see they exist?

The ability to work well within a team:
Do you get along well with others, and can you work effectively with them? Can you give and take accordingly and assume both a leader role and a follower role as the situation dictates?

The ability to work well independently:
Can you work well alone on assignments and projects? Do you need constant supervision and attention, or are you able to take an idea and run with it? Can you be trusted and counted on to get work done on your own?

Creativity and the ability to be an innovative thinker:
Can you think about things in new and different ways? Do you enjoy coming up with out-of-the-box solutions? Will you add additional insight to new and existing problems?

Leadership skills:
Are you a take-charge kind of person? Do you enjoy challenges? Are you comfortable taking the lead in a project or with a group?

Communication skills:
Are you able to effectively communicate both orally and in writing? Are you comfortable speaking in public and/or giving presentations? Can you clearly state an opinion, present some facts, defend an idea, and/or persuade a client via the written word?

Self-awareness:
Can you recognize when you need help? Are you cognizant of what you know and what you don't know? Are you connected to and mindful of your feelings and emotions?

WHAT ARE SOME TIPS FOR MAKING MY INTERNSHIP SUCCESSFUL?

Regardless of the kind of internship opportunity you seek and obtain, there are certain measures you can take to ensure that any type of experience is as successful and advantageous as it can be. Although no job is ideal, you can often turn even the most mediocre experience into a wonderful one by taking control of the situation and doing everything you can to make yourself a valuable addition to the company.

First and foremost, if you expect to be treated like a business professional, you need to act like one. Act the part and treat others as you wish to be treated. Enter into the internship with a positive attitude and maintain it throughout the course of the experience, even if the opportunity is different from what you thought it would be. Dress professionally. Because different companies have different cultures that affect the way their employees dress, err on the safe side and dress more conservatively than you think is necessary, at least to start. Once you have been in the position for a few weeks, you will have a better idea of what kind of dress code is expected and you can make whatever adjustments you feel are necessary. If ever in doubt, ask your supervisor. Be respectful to anyone remotely affiliated with the company. This includes the support staff, clients, customers, vendors, and friends. As an intern, you may understand the structure of the company from a big picture perspective, but you will not necessarily be aware of the nuances of the "social scene." Sometimes, the people who you think hold the least power can surprise you. For example, at one well-known consulting company, the floor receptionists are key decision-makers in determining which interns receive permanent job offers. Be nice to everyone and you won't have a problem. Follow all of the company rules and regulations that affect you. Being an intern does not exempt you from abiding by the policies of the organization. This is critically important when it comes to maintaining confidentiality. Most companies will have you sign a confidentiality agreement when you enter into an internship arrangement with them if you will be working with sensitive information, but regardless of whether or not you are asked to do this, you should always maintain the privacy of employees, clients, and customers within and outside of working hours.

Secondly, do your job and do it well. This means treating every assignment, task, and project as if it were the most important thing in the world. Be diligent and thorough. Follow through to completion as best you can on everything, no matter how trivial or menial you think it may be. If you need help, ask for it. Your supervisor would much rather take the time to answer your questions up front than take the time to fix your mistakes later on. As an intern, you are not expected to know how to do everything, so your supervisor will (or should) anticipate that you will need guidance, at least in the beginning. In other words, do not expect to know everything and understand that you will need help. Don't be ashamed of this, or embarrassed by it! Having said that, however, take note of the answers, suggestions, advice, and solutions you are given and try not to ask the same question twice. Listen carefully and take notes if you need to. Work smart and work hard. Guaranteed, your effort will be noticed and, most definitely, rewarded!

Thirdly, become the person that everyone wants to befriend. Kill them with kindness. Be enthusiastic and energetic. Look upon every task as a challenge and perform at the highest level you can. Work well with others and make sure you do what you can to make others see you as a valuable addition to the team. At the same time, be confident working on your own as well. Meet all of your deadlines and keep your supervisor and team members apprised of your progress on your assignments. Be flexible and adaptable to changes. Work situations are very rarely static. Priorities sometimes realign, deadlines often shift, and teams occasionally reassemble. Acknowledge your discomfort (if, in fact, you feel this way), but charge on ahead. Do what is asked of you without complaining and look upon every opportunity as a learning experience, for better or worse.

Use the three or four months of your internship as a period of time in which to hone your soft skills. To the extent you can, practice your communication and interpersonal skills. Observe those around you to see how conflicts are handled and how issues are resolved. Try to figure out the corporate culture and political atmosphere surrounding the company and determine how its employees work with (or against) each other in this type of environment. Build your self-confidence by asking for and completing projects successfully. Work on negotiating the differences between "hearing" and "listening." Show compassion and empathy for those you work with. Practice patience in situations that call for it. Motivate those around you by coming to work with a smile on your face and an enthusiasm for what you do. And, finally, become skilled in the art of self-reflection. Take note of what you like and what you don't like, what you are good at and what you are not so good at, and what changes you would make if you had the opportunity to do so.

By reflecting on the internship experience as a whole, and your specific role within it, you will be better able to figure out in which direction you wish to travel the next time around.

WHAT DO I DO WHEN MY INTERNSHIP ENDS?[2]

Let's assume you've made it through your first (or second, or third, or fourth) internship without a major hitch. It may not have been the perfect experience, but surely, it wasn't the worst. Now that it is over, you will want to take the following steps to officially end your role.

1. Say goodbye to everyone.
This seems blatantly obvious, but don't forget to say a heartfelt goodbye to everyone with whom you worked. This includes folks from the CEO to the mail worker, and everyone in between, if you had any contact with them at all during your stint. Thank them for their assistance and support during your time there.

2. Schedule a meeting with your supervisor, if one hasn't already been scheduled for you.
Most companies will want to conduct an exit interview with you, which is an opportunity for you to talk about your experience in depth. If your company does not regularly perform such meetings, ask for one. You will want to not only thank your supervisor for his or her guidance and direction, but also ask him or her for a personal and professional critique of your performance over the semester. Solicit advice and suggestions, ask about the possibility of a full-time job offer, and/or inquire about referrals to others in the field. You might also consider asking for a letter of reference/recommendation for future applications to other internships and jobs. Even if the experience was horrible (which is highly unlikely), you never want to burn a bridge because you never can assume what the future holds. Thank your supervisor for the opportunity, consider the internship a learning experience, and prepare more carefully for the next one.

3. Send thank-you notes to your supervisor, your teammates, and anyone else with whom you closely worked.
While it is nice to say goodbye in person, a hand written note is a classy touch and will most effectively showcase your gratitude for the opportunity.

---

[2] Adapted from "What to Do When the Internship Ends" by Michelle Tullier.

4. Update your resume soon after your internship ends.

You do not want to wait too long before doing this, as you don't want to forget the details of any of your assignments, projects, and most importantly, successful accomplishments. If you need help with specific phrasing and/or formatting, see your advisor or a counselor in your career services office.

5. Try to keep in touch with the people, or at least your direct supervisor, at the organization over the next year or so, especially if you are interested in pursuing a full-time position with the company in the future.

Even if they do not anticipate hiring you, they might be able to point you in the right direction towards other companies who have openings or towards other tools and resources that you may find valuable during your full-time job search. Send the occasional email, write a periodic note, stop by during a slow week, or pick up the phone and call. It never hurts to maintain contact with former employers, and, more often than not, it can actually help, especially in a tight job market and in a down economy.

And so, with this information to guide you on your way down the road towards internship success, I invite you to explore the Insider Internship Listings...

INSIDER

INTERNSHIP

LISTINGS

TABLE OF CONTENTS

SECTION TWO:
INSIDER INTERNSHIP LISTINGS

Note:

Intern Insider information is accurate as of the time of publication. Be sure to check the websites for organizations you may be interested in as additional positions and information may be posted.

AFLAC

Knowledge and skill building programs that help develop future careers.

Industry:
Insurance

State(s) in Which Internships are Offered:
Georgia

Monetary Compensation:
Yes

Compensation Structure for Internship Program:
Between $10 to $16 per hour

Intern Benefits:
• Complete housing assistance

Semesters that Internships are Offered:
Summer, Fall, Spring, Winter

Application Deadlines:
March 1st

→ PROGRAM OVERVIEW

Aflac's University Relations program focuses on building Aflac's brand on college campuses throughout the United States. We work with campus career counselors, professors and students to ensure they understand Aflac's internship and co-op opportunities. Internally, we partner with each business unit to gauge the business need in relation to opportunities for graduates. We then support the need by identifying sources of talent through college and university graduates. These efforts allow us to recruit and place top students for internships, co-ops and full-time opportunities.

→ PROGRAM DESCRIPTION

As companies get stronger and smarter about recruiting trends/methods, competition for great talent becomes reality. Recruiting young talent and mid-career professionals is a priority at Aflac and so is retaining the best talent that we have. We have created the University Relations Department, a division dedicated to recruiting undergraduate, graduate and MBA students. They partner directly with departments throughout the company to assess their hiring needs and to connect the appropriate applicant in a career they will excel. They also identify trends and best practices that will continue to make Aflac an employer of choice for top talent.

A jump-start to any career can begin with an internship or co-op program. A potential graduate can start learning about various career opportunities and gain valuable on-the-job experience. To be successful at Aflac, one must be able to fill the needs of customers in a professional manner and have a customer service mindset. Selected students will have opportunities to work under the direction of experienced personnel to gain knowledge and experience in preparation for professional opportunities within several areas such as information technology, marketing, finance or any other assigned business unit. They also will provide assistance on specific projects, many which are time-defined. Internists receive training and perform duties that help them become familiar with division functions, operations, management skills or style and internal company policies.

Aflac knows it is important to provide work/life benefits that fit the needs of the millennial generation. That's why we offer challenging and rewarding careers coupled with personal time off and community involvement.

We continuously make efforts to build strong relationships with our employees, customers and community. Aflac has been highlighted for workforce diversity, attention to working mothers, and credibility and respect towards our workforce. We have been recognized on *Fortune* magazine's list of the 100 Best Companies to Work For in America and *BusinessWeek* magazine as a Best Place to Launch a Career. The company's inclusion and opportunity efforts have also been recognized by *Black Enterprise* magazine as a Best Companies for Diversity and *Hispanic* magazine added it to its list of 100 Companies Providing the Most Opportunities to Hispanics. Women account for nearly 70 percent of all employees, with more than half in management and close to 30 percent in upper management. Minorities make up over 40 percent of the company and hold close to 24 percent of leadership positions.

→ PROGRAM UNIQUENESS

At Aflac, an internship is a 10-12 week, full-time, paid summer program where interns can be assigned to their area of interest (Marketing, Finance, Accounting, etc.) They will gain additional skills and knowledge about their future career choice and be able to interface with senior and executive-level management. Co-ops are 16-week work/school intervals that are geared toward students interested in an Information Technology profession. These full-time, paid positions allow students to complete one-semester of college, then co-op for one semester, etc. Corporate housing is also available for individuals outside of the metro-Columbus, GA area.

→ IDEAL CANDIDATE

Intern and co-op participants must currently be enrolled in an accredited college or university pursuing a bachelor's or master's degree in a specific field required by the participating division, such as accounting, information technology, marketing, or communications. Aflac seeks individuals who have committed to a major with a minimum GPA of 3.0

→ APPLICATION PROCESS

Students should prepare an updated resume along with a cover letter indicating their desire for an internship or co-op. Please visit aflac.com to find out additional information.

Contact Person: Keyla Cabret
Address: 1932 Wynnton Rd. Columbus, GA 31907
E-Mail Address: collegerecruiting@aflac.com
Phone Number: 706.323.3431
Website Address: www.aflac.com

ALASKA STATE PARKS

Volunteer Natural History interpreter for Alaska State Parks.

Industry: Government - State	
State(s) in Which Internships are Offered: Alaska	
Monetary Compensation: Yes	
Compensation Structure for Internship Program: $300 per month plus board	
Intern Benefits: • Complete housing assistance • Free parking • Training	
Semesters that Internships are Offered: Summer	
Application Deadlines: April 15	

→ **PROGRAM OVERVIEW**

The Alaska State Division of Parks and Recreation offers five natural history interpreter internship positions at Independence Mine State Historical Park and the Hatcher Pass Management Area.

→ **PROGRAM DESCRIPTION**

Hatcher Pass is high above the tree line in the Talkeetna Mountains and about 60 miles north of Anchorage. The Hatcher Pass road is a high-country route between the Matanuska and Susitna valleys. This is gold country, with several mines still in operation and much evidence of past mining activities.

Nestled in an alpine bowl at 3,500' elevation, Independence Mine's historic buildings date from Alaska's gold mining era. The buildings are partially restored for public tours and illustrate the history of prospecting and hard rock mining in Alaska. The park visitor center now occupies the old manager's house, built in the 1930s. Visitors to the park can enjoy a historic walking tour and beautiful alpine scenery. The area of responsibility includes the 48,000-acre Hatcher Pass East Management area, a mostly alpine, mountainous park.

The interpreters will provide guided one-hour tours of the historical park and surrounding area two to three times per day. Tours will focus on the historic buildings, but may also include the alpine tundra and the geology of the area. Interpreters will also share duties in the visitor center store operating the cash register, answering questions, and restocking inventory. Interpreters will receive thorough training on these topics prior to leading tours.

Some other duties include:

❖ Roving around the park to meet and greet visitors to provide them with historic and other information to further enhance their visit.

❖ Operating a cash register and maintaining the visitor center store.

❖ Participating in the general upkeep of the grounds and facilities on a daily basis.

❖ Assisting staff in special projects and/or the development of one or more displays related to the Independence Mine, or hard rock mining in general.

Some of the skills and qualities required for an intern are:

❖ The ability to work effectively with both a diverse staff and the public. We're looking for team players.

❖ Interest and ability in public speaking.

❖ The capacity to walk and stand for an entire shift.

❖ Experience with, or willingness to learn, cash register operations.

❖ An interest in history and/or mining.

It is also preferable that internship candidates have the ability to work closely with other people, the willingness to step in when needed, and the self-motivation to learn as much as possible about the area. You should be flexible, open-minded, enthusiastic, and have good organizational skills.

Compensation for interns is a small subsistence payment plus living quarters or RV space. We will be happy to assist you with volunteer internship requirements and paperwork.

→ PROGRAM UNIQUENESS

Independence Mine State Historical park is at 3,500' elevation and is in a beautiful mountain cirque.

→ IDEAL CANDIDATE

Candidates should be flexible, friendly, hard working, willing to learn, and should be able to get along well with others in a community and in a remote setting. Selection process is based on application, phone interview and professional reference checks.

→ APPLICATION PROCESS

Candidates who are selected from a pool of online applications will then interview over the phone. Professional reference checks will also be conducted.

Contact Person: Trish Herrmann

Address:
HC32 Box 6706
Wasilla, AK 99654

E-Mail Address:
trish.herrmann@alaska.gov

Phone Number:
907.745.0936 or 907.745.8907

Website Address:
www.dnr.state.ak.us/parks

ALIVE ARTS MEDIA

Create the media you wish to see.

Industry: Communications/Media Publishing/Print Media	
State(s) in Which Internships are Offered: Minnesota	
Monetary Compensation: No	
Intern Benefits: • Free Parking • Academic Credit	
Semesters that Internships are Offered: Summer Fall Spring	
Application Deadlines: Summer - March 27 Fall - July 12 Spring - November 13	

→ PROGRAM OVERVIEW

Alive Magazine is an on-line magazine created entirely by young women offering a creative and constructive outlet for today's youth to share stories of life experiences. The magazine is published by Alive Arts Media, Inc., a nonprofit organization that exists to empower young women in their creative, educational, and professional pursuits. Interns serve as short-term staff members with high levels of responsibility and input regarding organizational goals. Internships are available for women 25 and under in three departments, and positions are specialized according to each intern's strengths, interests, and career goals.

→ PROGRAM DESCRIPTION

Internships are available in three departments: Editorial, Graphic Design, and Public Relations. The Public Relations Department also includes Marketing and Advertising.

Editorial interns work closely with the Managing Editor to develop story packages, edit submissions, and produce two issues of our bi-monthly PDF publication, as well as weekly Web site content. Other projects include working with contributors to rewrite articles, recruiting writers and artists, developing internal guidelines and new programs, and writing for the magazine and Web site. Editorial interns should have experience writing and/or editing, preferably with a school publication or other organization. They must be highly motivated, organized, and have good interpersonal skills.

Graphic Design interns are responsible for designing layouts and coordinating artwork for at least two issues of *Alive Magazine* and the *Alive Magazine* Web site. They will also work with the Editorial team to develop new graphic elements, Web pages, and print materials as necessary. Other projects include developing our artist contributor database, coordinating photo shoots, and researching new design platforms and resources. There are also extensive opportunities available for interns with experience in Web design and development; please specify this interest in your cover letter. Graphic Design interns should be fluent in Adobe Creative Suite (we use InDesign to produce our PDF magazine, as well as PhotoShop, Illustrator, and Bridge). We are also looking for photographic skills (digital and/or 35 mm) and a strong multimedia portfolio, including print and Web design experience. Interns must be highly motivated, organized, and enthusiastic about working with a growing non-profit organization. Web design/development applicants must have working knowledge of CSS, PHP, HTML, and Flash or Ajax, with examples included in portfolio.

Public Relations interns work on projects ranging from advertising sales to developing partnerships with like-minded organizations. Public Relations interns also work to plan fundraisers and outreach events, write and distribute press releases, and set up networking meetings. This internship requires a great deal of research, phone calls, and problem solving! Interns will also have a chance to participate in the creation of *Alive Magazine*, and will gain a sense of the inner workings of magazine publishing and non-profit management. Public Relations interns should have strong writing, phone, sales, and networking skills. Public Relations interns should also be highly motivated, organized, and able to work on long-term projects independently.

➜ PROGRAM UNIQUENESS
When you begin your job search, organizations will want to know that you are experienced in your field. By interning with Alive Arts Media, you will receive quality experience that cannot compare to other internships. By being an integral part of the staff producing *Alive Magazine*, you will be entrusted with greater responsibilities than many interns at other organizations.

➜ IDEAL CANDIDATE
Interns must be 25 or under and able to work part-time hours in our Minneapolis office. Successful applicants are those who demonstrate a sincere passion for our mission and have the ability to work independently on major projects. Please see the Program Description for specific requirements for each department.

➜ APPLICATION PROCESS
To apply, email a cover letter, resume, and link to online portfolio (for design applicants) to apply@alivemagazine.org. Cover letters may be addressed to Jennifer Dotson, Executive Director. Please include which department you would like to be considered for. Selected applicants will be asked to interview at our office in Minneapolis.

Contact Information:

Address:
1720 Madison Street NE
Suite 300
Minneapolis, MN 55413

E-Mail Address:
info@alivemagazine.org

Phone Number:
612.284.4080

Website Address:
www.alivemagazine.org/internships

AMWAY

This paid internship offers practical, real world projects including a mentor.

Industry:
Manufacturing
State(s) in Which Internships are Offered:
California, Michigan
Monetary Compensation:
Yes
Compensation Structure for Internship Program:
Hourly rate averages $16 per hour for undergrad and varies for graduate students. In addition, $400 per month housing allowance in MI and $950 per month in CA.
Intern Benefits:
• Partial Housing Assistance
• Fitness Center Membership
• 50% discount at Company Store
• Toastmasters Membership
Semesters that Internships are Offered:
Summer
Application Deadlines: 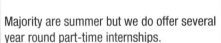
Applications are reviewed starting in October for positions in the spring.
Majority are summer but we do offer several year round part-time internships.

→ **PROGRAM OVERVIEW**

Each intern is given a specific project to work on. The project is designed to provide the intern with a breadth of learning and real-world experience. The main purpose of Amway's internship program is to identify future full-time talent. On average, we employ 110 interns in areas ranging from general business, finance, tax, supply chain, natural science, engineering, R&D, marketing, communications, IT, HR, and operations.

→ **PROGRAM DESCRIPTION**

Here is what interns have said they value about their experience at Amway:

❖ All internships are paid.

❖ All interns are eligible to receive either a housing allowance or a gas allowance if they live further than 50 miles from the facility.

❖ Internship opportunities are offered in both California and Ada, Michigan.

❖ Interns receive a 50% discount at company store.

❖ Interns have access to our Optimal You Fitness Facility, which includes weight room, cardio room, basketball court, fitness classes, and sponsored activities.

❖ This internship program provides the opportunity to develop a solid network of both professionals within the organization and other student interns.

❖ This program also allows interns to develop and broaden the transferable skills, such as leadership and teamwork, required in a workplace environment.

❖ Intern mentors are a great way to learn your way around the company and get feedback in real time.

→ **PROGRAM UNIQUENESS**

We provide the interns with an opportunity to network with all levels of management. We also have scheduled meetings in which executives will share their experiences and corporate direction. The interns are also assigned a mentor who provides one-on-one guidance and feedback on their project. We also have a reverse career fair where the interns have an opportunity to discuss their projects with management from various departments. This gives the interns an opportunity to discuss their transferable skills. We convert, on average, 40% of our senior interns to full-time employees.

→ IDEAL CANDIDATE

Potential candidates should apply at career fairs or online at www.amway.com.

→ APPLICATION PROCESS

Once you apply online, your resume will be reviewed by the hiring team. If your skill sets match the project, you will be called for an interview. You can also apply in person at the numerous career fairs or university events we attend.

Contact Person: Kevin Douglas

Address:
7575 Fulton Street East
Mail Code 78-1m
Ada, MI 49355

E-Mail Address:
kevin.douglas@amway.com

Phone Number:
616.787.1463

Website Address:
www.amway.com

ATK TACTICAL PROPULSION AND CONTROLS

A well-rounded, fulfilling, professional, strategic, progressive and life-changing experience.

Industry:	
Manufacturing	
State(s) in Which Internships are Offered:	
California	
Maryland	
Minnesota	
Tennessee	
Utah	
West Virginia	
Monetary Compensation:	
Yes	
Compensation Structure for Internship Program:	
Hourly compensation based on level in college. Ranges from $11.00 through $21.00	
Intern Benefits:	
• Complete housing assistance	
• Transportation stipend	
• Fitness Center Membership	
Semesters that Internships are Offered:	
Summer, Fall, Spring, Winter	
Application Deadlines:	
Requisitions are posted in December and all job offers are made by the end of February. Internship cohorts only start in June and successful candidates can work throughout the school year.	

→ PROGRAM OVERVIEW

The internship program is structured so that all interns are able to see how the entire manufacturing facility operates, receive hands-on training, and have the ability to not only develop themselves technically and as leaders, but grow personally as well.

→ PROGRAM DESCRIPTION

The internship program begins the first Monday in June and runs through the last week in August. We have the ability and option to keep interns on throughout their fall and spring semester if they are working in the local area and it fits within their school schedule. Interns go through an intense Orientation Day which is conducted by previous interns. Orientation consists of plant safety, wellness and fitness, corporate and plant law, payroll, business systems, plant organization, roles and responsibilities, and detailed explanation of the internship program. The interns will elect their own governing body which consists of a President, Vice President, and Recording Secretary. They also are required to form several small committees, each with a chair and co-chair. The internship program also consists of a required community service activity throughout the summer. At the end of the internship program, each intern is required to present their Goals and Initiatives to the plant executive leadership team. Throughout the summer, interns get on-the-job training, cross-training throughout the plant, weekly intern meetings with the entire intern body that includes training, customer and vendor visibility, and executive visibility. At the end of a very successful summer, the internship program closes with an intern picnic.

→ PROGRAM UNIQUENESS

We truly believe in giving interns the opportunity to grow, develop themselves and continue employment with us until they are ready to retire. That being said, we do everything in our power to provide them with the tools and techniques that they need to mature, grow and add value to the organization. Our interns are developed from the time they arrive until the time they leave. We host interns from all over the country and there is a lot of professional and personal integration so that the intern body feels like a family. We strongly believe in giving back to the community, and we have built that philosophy into our intern program. Interns are required to do multiple community service projects while they are working with us throughout the summer. Some interns lead the project and others work the project. The interns also lead themselves. We provide coaching and mentoring to their governing body, but in essence they are building and developing themselves as leaders, handling day-to-day crises that arise, and leading all training and development initiatives.

→ IDEAL CANDIDATE

Candidates must have completed their Freshman year. Requisitions are posted based on business need and applicants are screened based on degree, level, GPA and any work experience they may have had. Once the candidate's resume is screened successfully, they are contacted to conduct a telephone interview between the hiring manager and the Human Resources department. If the phone interview is successful, then the offer is made contingent upon a drug screen and a background check.

→ APPLICATION PROCESS

Applicants complete a profile on our website and then apply for all requisitions that are of interest to them. When they apply, the resume they have used in their profile is automatically loaded. Once the candidate's resume is screened successfully, they are contacted to conduct a telephone interview between the hiring manager and the Human Resources department. If the phone interview is successful, then the offer is made contingent upon a drug screen and a background check.

Contact Person: Gretta L. Ramsey

Address:
210 State Road 956
Rocket Center, WV 26726

E-Mail Address:
gretta.ramsey@atk.com

Phone Number:
304.726.5074

Website Address:
www.atk.com

AVIS BUDGET GROUP

Avis Budget Group Summer/ Year-Long Internship Program – Based in Parsippany, NJ

Industry: Transportation	
State(s) in Which Internships are Offered: New Jersey	
Monetary Compensation: Yes	
Compensation Structure for Internship Program: Compensation is based on the school year of the incoming intern.	
Intern Benefits: • Free Parking • Fitness Center Membership	
Semesters that Internships are Offered: Summer Fall Spring Winter	
Application Deadlines: Rolling deadline	

→ **PROGRAM OVERVIEW**

Avis Budget Group operates two of the most recognized brands in the global vehicle rental industry through Avis and Budget. Avis is a leading rental car supplier to the premium commercial and leisure segments of the travel industry. Budget is a leading rental car supplier to the price-conscious segments of the industry.

→ **PROGRAM DESCRIPTION**

The summer program is a paid internship that will be hosted at the corporate headquarters in Parsipanny, New Jersey. Interns will be responsible for their transportation and housing arrangements. Interns must be available to work full-time throughout the entire length of the internship program. During the program, interns will be provided with a challenging, educational and rewarding experience that includes (but is not limited to): assisting in the day-to-day operations of the assigned department, working on department projects, mentoring, attending development workshops, and participating in company-sponsored team-building events.

→ **PROGRAM UNIQUENESS**

We offer various team-building events throughout the year, which include:

❖ Ice Cream Social led by senior interns.

❖ Lunch 'n' Learns.

❖ Senior Leadership Team hosted lunch.

❖ Group intern lunches.

❖ Training classes (Improving Personal Productivity, for example).

❖ Participation in the performance management process.

❖ Training on our performance management system.

❖ 8-10 minute intern presentations in front of their peers, mentors, managers, department heads, etc.

❖ Interns are assigned both a manager and a mentor.

→ IDEAL CANDIDATE

Interested applicants must have the following eligibility requirements to be considered:

❖ Enrolled at an accredited university

❖ Cumulative GPA of 3.0 or higher

❖ Majoring in a business-related discipline

❖ Eager to learn

❖ A self-starter

→ APPLICATION PROCESS

Candidates will be asked to submit their resumes online. They will then go through a phone screen process and complete an in-person application and interview(s).

Contact Person: Mimi Rodriguez

Address:
6 Sylvan Way
Parsippany, NJ 07054

E-Mail Address:
mimi-rodriquez@avisbudget.com

Phone Number:
973.496.4229

Website Address:
www.avisbudgetgroup.com/careers

BEST BUY

Have Fun While Being the Best!

Industry: Retail/Merchandising	
State(s) in Which Internships are Offered: Minnesota	
Monetary Compensation: Yes	
Compensation Structure for Internship Program: Interns are paid hourly	
Intern Benefits: • Complete housing assistance • Transportation stipend • Free parking	
Semesters that Internships are Offered: Summer	
Application Deadlines: The intern application period runs from January to February	

→ PROGRAM OVERVIEW

Summer is an exciting time to do something new, fun and challenging. Like preparing for your future career! The Best Buy Corporate Summer Internship Program is a great opportunity for enrolled college students like you to gain some invaluable work experience. Held at our corporate campus in Richfield, Minnesota, you will interact with company executives from different departments and participate in a series of activities that will expose you to the multi-faceted world of consumer electronics retailing. Your internship could also be the beginning of a rewarding career for you at Best Buy.

→ PROGRAM DESCRIPTION

The Best Buy Summer Internship Program kicks off between mid-May and the beginning of June (there are multiple start dates) and continues through mid-August. Typically the program is 10 to 12 weeks long. The number of interns Best Buy hires is determined by the needs of the business. The Corporate University Relations Program starts recruiting talented interns during the spring semester. There will be positions posted on our website and in career centers at schools across the country from January through mid-April. New intern positions are continually posted, so please check back often. Each posting will have an application deadline along with a specific set of criteria that must be met for consideration.

→ PROGRAM UNIQUENESS

Location:

The Best Buy corporate campus is located near the Twin Cities of Minneapolis and St. Paul, Minnesota. With more than 10,000 lakes, a vibrant arts community, professional sports teams, the Mall of America and various attractions to visit, the area is guaranteed to entertain you.

Employee Discount:

As a Best Buy intern, you'll be able to use your employee discount on the newest and coolest technology sold in our stores.

Salary and Travel Assistance:

Best Buy internships are competitively paid. Out-of-state interns will receive housing and travel assistance.

The Best Buy University Relations Team:

The team hosts various intern events during the summer. You will also participate in programs held by MIX (mixtc.org), where you'll network with interns from other companies in the Twin Cities. Additional activities include leadership roundtables with executive officers and a competitive, summer-long internship project that requires you to work in teams tackling a company initiative.

→ IDEAL CANDIDATE AND APPLICATION PROCESS

Each posting will have an application deadline along with a specific set of criteria that must be met for consideration. To view the internship postings on our website, create a profile and apply:

❖ Access http://careers.bestbuy.com

❖ At the bottom of the page, select Student and Entry Level positions

❖ Scroll down to view the internship postings

❖ Apply for the internship(s) you are interested in

If you have any questions, please contact the Best Buy University Relations Team at: university.relations@bestbuy.com

Contact Information:

Address:
7601 Penn Avenue S
Richfield, MN 55423

E-Mail Address:
university.relations@bestbuy.com

Phone Number:
612.291.1000

Website Address:
www.bestbuy.com

BOSTON MAGAZINE

Become an expert on Boston news and arts and culture with *Boston* magazine's internship program.

Industry:
Communications/Media
- Journalism

State(s) in Which Internships are Offered:
Massachusetts

Monetary Compensation:
None

Compensation Structure for Internship Program:
N/A

Intern Benefits:
• Internship may be done for credit with school's permission

Semesters that Internships are Offered:
Summer
Fall
Spring

Application Deadlines:
Nov. 18 - winter, May 15 - summer

→ PROGRAM OVERVIEW

Boston magazine is an award-winning city magazine that covers Boston with superlative expository features, narratives, profiles, and unsurpassed service journalism including travel, fashion, beauty, best-in-town dining criticism, and arts and entertainment. Founded in 1961, it has a circulation of 125,000 and about 500,000 monthly readers. The website receives an average of 175,000 unique visitors each month and as many as 700,000 page views each month.

→ PROGRAM DESCRIPTION

Boston magazine interns do not make copies and get coffee. Our interns work as a team on at least one major research project. Each is assigned to a senior editor or writer to help as a research assistant on major stories. And almost without exception, each will write bylined articles for publication. Interns also do fact checking and learn other facets of publishing. Research assignments are an integral and important part of this internship. This research is no different than that conducted by full-time staff. We insist that it be done accurately and with attention to detail.

We require that interns make a serious, concerted effort to treat this internship as they would a paid position. We do not accept loose schedules, tardiness, or a minimal work ethic. If you are looking to breeze your way through an internship, this is not the place for you. The work we give interns holds the same weight as work we give our top editors, and we expect the same level of quality and commitment.

The editorial web interns will also learn the day-to-day basics of running the daily website for *Boston* magazine, which includes uploading content (articles, photo galleries, events, and listings for restaurants, shops, and other local businesses), as well as updating site modules on a daily basis. They will also master the use of keywords for search engine optimization, and learn how to create email newsletters, and how to use blogging software.

→ PROGRAM UNIQUENESS

Interns are treated like they are members of the *Boston* magazine staff. Students will be totally immersed in the news and arts and entertainment culture of Boston. They'll be the first to know what's going on around town, be able to write about it, and see their work published in the magazine and on the web almost instantaneously.

→ IDEAL CANDIDATE

Candidates should be enrolled in college, have participated in journalism and/or writing courses, and be interested in learning about magazines and websites.

→ APPLICATION PROCESS

Students will submit a cover letter and resume, along with several published writing samples, as well as links to their online work (if available). The chosen candidates will then be interviewed in person or by phone by *Boston* magazine editors.

Contact Persons:
Rachel Baker, Jamie Coelho,
Jason Schwartz, Brigid Sweeney

Address:
300 Massachusetts Ave.
Boston, MA 02115

E-Mail Address:
Internships@Bostonmagazine.com

Phone Number:
617.262.9700

Website Address:
www.bostonmagazine.com

BOY SCOUTS OF AMERICA

Hands-on experience for interns in executive work.

Industry:
Not-For-Profit

State(s) in Which Internships are Offered:
All 50 states + District of Columbia

Monetary Compensation:
Yes

Compensation Structure for Internship Program:
Compensation varies based on each autonomous local BSA council office; usually hourly or stipend for the semester

Intern Benefits:
• Free Parking
• Learning that will enhance academic and professional experiences

Semesters that Internships are Offered:
Summer
Fall
Spring
Winter

Application Deadlines:
Varies by each of the 300 local BSA council offices

→ PROGRAM OVERVIEW
BSA's local college internship program is designed to be a unique, educational work and interpersonal relationship program especially and specifically designed to increase practical knowledge of the role and responsibilities of an executive opportunity. Students receive another opportunity to extend their network through volunteer and professional relationships. BSA's local council internship program for college students provides an opportunity to develop a pool of experienced professionals.

→ PROGRAM DESCRIPTION
BSA's local council internship program consists of one full spring, summer, or fall semester. A minimum 20-hour week is required, including evening and weekend meetings and activities. Only first- and second-semester senior students are eligible. The internship program is open to all academic majors, but liberal arts and human service areas seem more conducive to a career in Scouting. Examples of three of the many types of internships are listed below.

Philanthropy/Finance:
Interns will receive practical experience in a variety of areas related to financing in the local council.

Membership Development:
Interns will learn about organizing new groups. They will also learn about the chartered organization concepts of the Boy Scouts of America (BSA) as they learn how to organize, recruit, and retain members.

Volunteerism:
The lifeblood of the BSA is its volunteers. Interns will learn:

❖ Who volunteers

❖ How to recruit them

❖ Where to recruit them

❖ Why people are the valued component of Scouting

→ PROGRAM UNIQUENESS
Mentors assigned to interns will:

❖ Develop a working relationship with the intern and be enthusiastic, positive, and understanding.

❖ Provide two hours of training each week.

❖ Take the necessary time to explain assignments and their importance.

❖ Turn in evaluations on time and assist the intern in completing evaluations.

❖ Assist the intern with his or her weekly schedule to include 20 hours of work for the council.

❖ Include the intern in as many council or district functions as possible, including staff meetings.

❖ Keep the immediate supervisor informed of the intern's progress.

❖ Be a role model.

❖ If applicable, assist the intern in completing an application for full-time placement.

→ IDEAL CANDIDATE

First-semester senior students are preferred. Approved interns must subscribe to the values of the Scout Oath and Scout Law, and must register as adult members of the BSA. Commitment of a full semester (12 to 16 weeks) is required.

→ APPLICATION PROCESS

Though it differs geographically, interns contact and apply to the local council where they are interested in interning.

Contact Person: Carolyn Altemus

Address:
1325 W. Walnut Hill Lane
P.O. Box 152079
Irving, TX 75019-2079

E-Mail Address:
caltemus@netbsa.org

Phone Number:
972.580.2118

Website Address:
www.scouting.org

CARGILL

Apply knowledge gained in the classroom to a real-life environment.

Industry: Agribusiness, Food, and Risk Management	
State(s) in Which Internships are Offered: Various locations within the United States.	
Monetary Compensation: Yes	
Compensation Structure for Internship Program: Will be different per function (i.e. HR, I/T, Engineering, etc.)	
Intern Benefits: • Partial housing assistance • Partial relocation assistance	
Semesters that Internships are Offered: Summer, Fall, Spring, Winter	
Application Deadlines: Open until all positions are filled.	

→ PROGRAM OVERVIEW

Cargill, founded in 1865, is an international provider of food, agricultural and risk management products and services. With customers spanning the globe, we provide expert advice in crops and livestock; food; health and pharmaceuticals; industrial; and financial and risk management. Cargill now employs over 160,000 people in 67 countries around the world.

Our Vision Statement: Our Purpose is to be the global leader in nourishing people. Our mission is to create distinctive value. Our approach is to be trustworthy, creative and enterprising. Our measures are engaged employees, satisfied customers, enriched communities and profitable growth.

→ PROGRAM DESCRIPTION

Whatever job you're looking for, you can probably find it at Cargill. Our diverse partnerships across a variety of industries mean countless career opportunities for you. It's your choice. It's your future. And you can make it happen at Cargill.

Work will be complimented by a quality approach to supervision and mentorship. An on-going job performance assessment will be provided. Opportunity to learn more about Cargill's diverse businesses through events such as first day orientation, local site visits, as well as the Intern Forum Event.

Experiences may include the following:

- **Business Manager Intern:**
  Accountable for a wide variety of challenging aspects of the business, including revenue and profit growth, employee engagement, talent development and business support.

- **I/T:**
  Work on small teams with other interns on two different challenges. Challenges could include project management, business analysis, application support, application development, database administration, business process re-engineering, network and systems management, as well as many others.

- **Engineering:**
  Gain an understanding of the plant, process, and equipment by working with a diverse group of functional areas on such projects as efficiency issues, working with contractors, energy-related process improvements, and plant improvements.

- **Finance/Accounting:**
Assigned project work with cross-functional teams, daily work similar to that of an entry-level accountant or financial analyst, and be able to present what they worked on and learned at Cargill at the end of their internship.

- **HR:**
Experiences in one of three areas: the corporate office, a business unit, or a plant location with specific assignments in compensation, benefits, talent recruiting, or learning and performance management.

- **Quality Assurance Chemist:**
Provide analytical support to process, and ensure conformance to customer requirements for quality and food safety.

- **Production Supervisor:**
Provide production management skills in the daily operation of an export grain elevator or foodservice packaging plant.

- **Commodity Merchant:**
Build relationships with internal and external customers in order to successfully buy, sell, and trade commodities and the by-products of each.

- **Farm Marketer Trainee:**
Working with grain producers on various projects in the agricultural sales and marketing area in order to build long-term relationships with our customers.

- **Plant Manager:**
Manage the facilities and the people to produce animal nutrition products as efficiently as possible while meeting all of Cargill Animal Nutrition, corporate and government guidelines.

- **Operations Manager Trainee:**
Assist with facility operations and personnel to maximize efficiencies, operate within applicable government regulations, and assist in identifying and developing customer solutions and service.

➜ IDEAL CANDIDATE
Internships are open to sophomores, juniors, or seniors currently enrolled in an accredited college or university academic program. Overall 3.0 GPA preferred. Candidates must have the right to work in the U.S. that is not based solely on possession of a student visa or a visa sponsored by a third-party employer.

➜ APPLICATION PROCESS
Candidates must apply directly to the posting on our website at www.ichoosecargill.com.

Resume is required when applying. A 30-minute interview will be conducted either on campus or over the phone. If recommended, the candidate will receive an offer for a co-op or summer internship.

Contact Information:
Website Address: www.ichoosecargill.com

CARPENTER ST. CROIX VALLEY NATURE CENTER

CNC provides opportunities to grow & learn in nature through internships.

Industry:	
Environment	
State(s) in Which Internships are Offered: 	
Minnesota	
Wisconsin	
Monetary Compensation:	
Yes	
Compensation Structure for Internship Program:	
Stipend of up to $150 per week	
Intern Benefits:	
• Complete housing assistance	
Semesters that Internships are Offered:	
Summer	
Fall	
Spring	
Winter	
Application Deadlines:	
Winter - Oct. 1	
Spring - Dec. 1	
Summer - Mar. 1	
Fall - June 1	

→ PROGRAM OVERVIEW

Looking for an outdoor experience that you'll never forget? Gain career skills while working in the great outdoors and doing what you love! Make the earth a better place by fostering a love of the outdoors in children and visitors of all ages or by conserving and preserving natural habitat. Enjoy the fruits of your labor by munching on an eco-friendly apple that you have helped to grow. Carpenter St. Croix Valley Nature Center is seeking interns in either Environmental Education or in Horticulture for every season. We want you on the team!

→ PROGRAM DESCRIPTION

Carpenter St. Croix Valley Nature Center (CNC) is a private non-profit nature center located 5 miles north of Hastings, MN on the scenic St. Croix River. Its mission is to develop and enhance appreciation for the natural world through quality environmental education, conservation practices, and outdoor experiences for visitors of all ages and capabilities. The site consists of some 720 acres of diverse habitats on both the Minnesota and the Wisconsin sides of the river including a hands-on Visitor Center and 15 miles of hiking trails.

Environmental Education Interns receive training from professional naturalists to teach a variety of programs to visitors of all ages and help with ongoing research projects. Interns play an important role in caring for and training program animals including raptors, reptiles and amphibians. Opportunities will be available to learn new techniques for developing and evaluating new programs as well as developing public exhibits and educational displays.

Horticulture Interns receive training from professional horticulturists, help with the apple orchard utilizing Integrated Pest Management, assist with the many gardens at the Center, play an active role in prairie restoration, and become involved in all horticulture activities as they arise.

Because CNC is a small organization dedicated to sharing its mission, interns are invited to take part in all activities the center has to offer and to gain additional skills outside of their internship. In addition, interns at CNC are expected to design and complete an individual project of their choice to be used at CNC in the future. A recent intern writes, *"The internship here at Carpenter Nature Center has been an amazing experience. I have learned new things not only about wildlife, but also about myself and my abilities. This internship has furthered my desire to enter this field and given me the opportunity to prove to myself and find that I can do it and do it well."*

→ PROGRAM UNIQUENESS

Interns gain personal and professional skills by working closely with staff in either Environmental Education or Horticulture through hands-on education, an open atmosphere, directed work experiences, a variety of daily activities, and exposure to new challenges.

→ IDEAL CANDIDATE

Carpenter Nature Center is seeking interns who have a desire to pursue a career in either Environmental Education or in Horticulture, have a general knowledge of natural history, have an ability to relate well to all kinds of people, are self-motivated and reliable, and have excellent written and oral communication skills.

→ APPLICATION PROCESS

To apply, send completed application (available at www.CarpenterNatureCenter.org), letter of intent, and current resume to:

Intern Coordinator
Carpenter St. Croix Valley Nature Center
12805 St. Croix Trail
S. Hastings, MN USA 55033

or email to:
michelle@CarpenterNatureCenter.org

Applications will be processed upon receipt. On-site or phone interview may follow.

Contact Person: Intern Coordinator

Address:
12805 St. Croix Trail S
Hastings, MN 55033

E-Mail Address:
michelle@carpenterNatureCenter.org

Phone Number:
651.437.4359

Website Address:
www.CarpenterNatureCenter.org

CATO INSTITUTE

Explore public policy while furthering the cause of liberty.

Industry:	
Not-For-Profit	

State(s) in Which Internships are Offered:
District of Columbia

Monetary Compensation:
Yes

Compensation Structure for Internship Program:
$700 a month stipend for full-time internships paid in two monthly installments. Law students receive specific legal work as well as a different stipend. Part-time interns (permitted in exceptional cases) receive a pro-rated stipend.

Intern Benefits:
None

Semesters that Internships are Offered:
Year round

Application Deadlines:
Online application
(http://www.cato.org/jobs/intern/)
must be received by:

- July 1 for the fall semester; notification by August 1
- November 1 for the spring semester; notification by December 1
- March 1 for the summer; notification by April 15.

→ PROGRAM OVERVIEW

Cato interns assist policy staff as researchers; work with the conference department to organize policy conferences, debates, and forums; attend seminars and conferences; and assist

Application Deadlines: (cont.):
To allow for visa and travel arrangements, international applicants' application forms and autobiographies must be received by:

- June 1 for fall semester; notification by July 1
- October 1 for the spring semester; notification by November 1
- February 1 for the summer; notification by April 1.

Internship program starting and ending dates:

Fall: Early September to late December
Spring: Early January to late May
Summer: Early June to late August

Cato's professional staff by copying and filing newspaper articles, distributing materials to congressional offices, and preparing mailings.

In addition to their research and other duties, interns take part in regular seminars on politics, economics, law, and philosophy, as well as a series of lectures and films on libertarian themes. (Summer interns are also encouraged, but not required, to play on the Institute's softball team.) Cato internships are for undergraduates (regardless of major), recent graduates, graduate students, or law students who have a strong commitment to individual liberty, free markets, limited government, and peace.

→ PROGRAM DESCRIPTION

The Cato Institute is a public policy research organization whose publications and conferences since 1977 have presented market-liberal solutions for the full range of policy issues. Cato's objective is to reawaken interest in America's founding ideals: personal liberty, private property, free markets, free trade, limited government, and nonintervention in foreign affairs. The Institute is named for Cato's Letters, libertarian essays that were widely read in the

American colonies in the 18th century and that played a major role in laying the philosophical foundation for the American Revolution.

There is a wide variety of departments in which interns work at the Cato Institute. Policy areas include such subjects as health care and entitlements reform, constitutional law, energy policy, and foreign and military policy. Interns assist department directors and research assistants with research and data collection. Some interns are assigned to the Media Relations and Development departments, where they get hands-on experience working with journalists and donors, respectively. We do our best to align interns and their preferences. All interns fulfill such responsibilities as clerical work, delivery of studies to Capitol Hill, and setting up for Cato events, including registering guests and carrying hand-held microphones at public forums and debates. All interns take active part in weekly seminars and research and writing workshops.

→ PROGRAM UNIQUENESS

Not only are interns assigned to work on research and administrative projects for our various policy departments, they also attend a series of research seminars. Cato policy experts and visiting scholars address Cato interns and new staff two or three times per week on topics ranging from global warming and energy policy to intellectual history. In addition, Cato interns attend workshops on writing and public speaking. The historical and theoretical overview of liberalism provided by the Cato Institute's core curriculum is offered by very few organizations worldwide. Such thorough investigation of classical liberal scholarship is available on only a handful of campuses with a handful of professors and through three or four other organizations dedicated to advancing classical liberal scholarship. The opportunity to participate in the academic portion of Cato's internship program itself is a valuable experience. Interns walk away from this program armed with the intellectual tools needed to defend peace, voluntarism, and tolerance in just about every realm of human society. While the career-focused skills of research and writing could be replicated elsewhere, in only a few other institutions are such skills taught within the very specific context of advancing individual liberty, free markets, and peace. It is the passion for liberty combined with the research and communications expertise that make the career skills workshops in the internship curriculum unique. The film seminar series, which highlights documentaries, television series, and feature films that provoke discussion related to other parts of the Cato curriculum, is also unrivaled in most places in the world. Interns gather for the film seminar series having already read an accompanying selection of articles and essays. After the viewing, interns gather with their discussion leader to explore the various liberty-related themes and economic principles illustrated in the chosen film.

→ IDEAL CANDIDATE/ APPLICATION PROCESS

All intern applicants must complete the online application found at:

http://www.cato.org/jobs/intern

Resumes, writing samples and letters of recommendation may be requested at a later date.

Contact Information	
Address:	
1000 Massachusetts Ave. NW Washington DC, 20001	
E-Mail Address:	
intern@cato.org	
Phone Number:	
202.789.5251	
Website Address:	
www.cato.org	

CDM

We provide our interns with experience, opportunity, challenge, mentorship, teamwork, learning, excellence, accomplishment, growth, and fun.

Industry:

Consulting/Environmental

State(s) in Which Internships are Offered:

Arizona, California, Colorado, Connecticut, Florida, Georgia, Illinois, Indiana, Kansas, Louisiana, Massachusetts, Michigan, Minnesota, Mississippi, Montana, New Hampshire, New Jersey, New York, North Carolina, Ohio, Pennsylvania, Rhode Island, South Carolina, Texas, Virginia, Washington

Monetary Compensation:

Yes

Compensation Structure for Internship Program:

Salary range from $14-$20/hr depending upon year of graduation and degree level.

Intern Benefits:

• Accrued vacation after 6 months.
• Accrued sick time after 3 months.

Paid holidays Service Time - applied if students join the firm upon graduation.

Commuter Program - pre-tax benefits to various commuter options .

Capital Accumulation Plan - Students may contribute to a 401(k) plan after date of hire.

CDM will partially match 401(k) contributions and make profit-sharing contributions after 1 year of employment.

Semesters that Internships are Offered:

Summer, Fall, Spring Winter

Application Deadlines:
We hire students throughout the year, and each school maintains its own schedule for their respective co-op and internship programs. For summer, applications are preferred by the middle of March.

→ PROGRAM OVERVIEW
Are you ready? At CDM, we seek to employ the best professionals in the industry. We partner with educational institutions to enhance the student experience through our co-op & intern program. Co-ops and interns working toward their bachelor's, master's, and doctoral degrees join CDM at various stages of their education. We provide you with a meaningful and challenging work experience, mentoring by experienced professionals, and the opportunity to contribute to innovative projects that improve the environment and the communities in which we live.

→ PROGRAM DESCRIPTION
CDM was founded in 1947 with a focus on environmental services. Today, with more than 4,000 employees, CDM is a full-service consulting, engineering, construction, and operations firm delivering exceptional service to public and private clients worldwide. From drinking water supply and wastewater treatment to environmental management systems to transportation and industrial facilities design, we listen carefully to our clients, think about their best approach, and deliver a tailored solution.

In 2008, we hired 182 student employees throughout the year. Our student co-ops and interns maintain a high grade point average and are dedicated, enthusiastic, and excited about learning. Many of our students are leaders on and off campus. We look for co-ops and interns who want to make a tangible contribution to projects and are actively involved in professional and environmentally conscious organizations, such as Engineers Without Borders. Continuing involvement in community service is encouraged while working at CDM.

CDM hires co-ops and interns on a part- and full-time basis across a wide range of disciplines, such as air quality, civil, environmental, chemical, electrical, construction, geotechnical, mechanical, structural, instrumentation, water resources and transportation engineers; geologists, hydro-geologists, environmental scientists and GIS/information management; human resources; and marketing. CDM has more than 100 offices worldwide, with our co-ops and interns working mainly in our many U.S. locations side-by-side with talented CDM employees. Our student employees have the opportunity to network across the firm with professionals ranging from other co-ops and interns to recent graduates and experienced staff. CDM strives to help its co-ops and interns become an integral part of the organization, offering increased levels of responsibility based on experience and performance.

It is our experience that most of our student employees receive college credit for their work with the firm. Your ability to receive credit for your time at CDM depends on your school's co-op and intern regulations. Check with the career center on your campus for more information. CDM has a strong history of employing our co-ops and interns in full-time positions after graduation. Many of our students return to CDM over the course of their student careers and may be able to work in different locations or positions, depending upon the current openings in our offices. We hope the work experience our co-ops and interns have sparks an interest in the organization and for the future. This program is a unique opportunity to take a first-hand look at what it is like to work for CDM. Are you ready?

→ PROGRAM UNIQUENESS

During your internship or co-op position with us, we understand that you want to contribute real value to the organization. We applaud your initiative! Unique to CDM is helping each student manage their career by clearly defining learning outcomes prior to their start date. What are your personal, professional, and educational goals? How can we help you meet them? During your very first week, you and your manager will discuss these goals and establish outcomes, which are later measured and evaluated by you to determine the next steps in your career.

→ IDEAL CANDIDATE

CDM employs a wide range of co-ops and interns at all stages of their education, including students seeking their bachelor's, master's, and doctoral degrees. Our students maintain a high grade point average and are leaders on and off campus. We look for students who want to contribute to projects and who are dedicated, enthusiastic, and excited about learning.

→ APPLICATION PROCESS

All current co-op and intern positions are posted online at www.cdm.com/careers. In support of CDM's sustainability practices, we do not accept paper resumes but only those submitted electronically. Students may submit to specific positions or post their resume for future consideration. Resumes are reviewed by recruiters and applicants will be contacted based on the availability of openings aligned with qualifications.

Contact Information:

Address:
50 Hampshire Street
1 Cambridge Place
Cambridge, MA 02139

Website Address:
www.cdm.com

CHROMOCELL CORPORATION

Grow with a team enabling drug discovery with proprietary technology.

Industry: Biotechnology	
State(s) in Which Internships are Offered: New Jersey	
Monetary Compensation: Yes	
Compensation Structure for Internship Program: Compensation varies dependent upon experience.	
Intern Benefits: • Free parking • Possible future full time positions • Continuing education programs • Involvement with the company development through weekly meetings • Food • Parking	
Semesters that Internships are Offered: Summer, Fall, Spring, Winter	
Application Deadlines: We currently do not have specific application deadlines, as recruitment depends on our various needs.	

→ PROGRAM OVERVIEW

Challenge, mentorship and growth are just a few words that will describe your Chromocell experience. Founded in 2003 by Dr. Kambiz Shekdar and Nobel Laureate Dr. Gunter Blobel, Chromocell is a biotechnology company engaged in drug discovery and development through research. As an intern at Chromocell, you will have a unique opportunity to learn, as well as truly contribute to the growth of a fast-paced drug discovery company. Take this opportunity to demonstrate your strong initiative and work ethic to push Chromocell forward and kick start your career.

→ PROGRAM DESCRIPTION

Chromocell is a biotechnology company commercializing a novel technology that significantly accelerates drug discovery and development. Chromocell creates cell lines and cell-based assays that enable drug targets that were previously unreachable or unobtainable.

Each year, Chromocell offers a limited number of outstanding students the opportunity to participate in the company's internship program. Our program is geared toward highly talented and motivated students looking for a part-time position that is intellectually challenging and offers insight into the workings of biotechnology. The program consists of an initial trial period followed by a comprehensive training program in cell culture and general lab techniques. Some of the techniques you can expect to learn are the culture and handling of a variety of mammalian cells, or using aseptic techniques that include passaging, freezing and thawing. Through this work, you will be exposed to a variety of instrumentation such as electronic cell counters, micro-plate imaging systems, centrifuges, and a variety of electronic pipettes. Interns will also be involved in various tasks that keep any lab running smoothly, such as monitoring lab inventory, sterilizing labware and maintaining a clean and efficient work area.

Working at Chromocell will afford you many benefits for your future endeavors. You will have gained technical experience and theoretical skills such as the scientific method and problem solving which you can apply to a variety of future jobs, or use during graduate school. Working at Chromocell will also help you build contacts within the research community that may be used as references or resources for future jobs. Interns who have remained with the company for more than one year and proven themselves as strong members of the team may be afforded the opportunity to be intricately involved in research projects within the company; this may involve cross-training on new techniques with departments other than the cell culture group. Highly successful interns may be considered for full-time employment.

Our interns play a key role in the success of our operations by providing support for all projects at the company. Working within Chromocell, you will be among many highly talented and motivated scientists always willing to take time to share their scientific expertise with you. Currently, our company has over a dozen interns from a neighboring university. We are highly selective and look for the best and brightest. We welcome applicants with a strong drive to achieve goals and exceed expectations.

→ PROGRAM UNIQUENESS

Chromocell combines book-smarts in biology with the real world of biotechnology and drug discovery. You'll learn scientific techniques, background, and principles in a fast-paced environment while being exposed to cutting-edge technology and equipment. As part of the team, you'll have the chance to see all workings of the company by taking part in weekly lab meetings and project meetings, which will broaden and enrich your scientific experience. We have 24/7 operations, giving flexibility with scheduling between your classes and the chance for weekend work. Some interns have gained school credit via co-op programs, on top of receiving compensation!

→ IDEAL CANDIDATE

Prerequisites for applying to an internship at Chromocell include the following: Enrollment and exceptional academic achievement at a college/university, submission of a formal resume and cover letter, full interview with multiple Chromocell team members and a four-week probationary trial period.

→ APPLICATION PROCESS

Interns should apply with their resumes and cover letters. After these are reviewed, candidates selected to continue will be invited for an on-site interview with a variety of Chromocell team members. If invited to join Chromocell, the intern will undergo an initial four-week trial period, which allows both you and Chromocell to evaluate if the position is a good fit. After successful completion of the trial period, there will be a comprehensive training program in cell culture and general lab techniques.

Contact Information:

Address:
685 US Hwy. One
North Brunswick, NJ 08902

E-Mail Address:
info@chromocell.com

Phone Number:
732.565.1113

Website Address:
www.chromocell.com

COMMODORE BUILDERS

Hands-on experience in a dynamic construction environment.

Industry: Construction	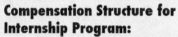
State(s) in Which Internships are Offered: Massachusetts	
Monetary Compensation: Yes	
Compensation Structure for Internship Program: Interns are paid at an hourly average rate of $15-$17 per hour.	
Semesters that Internships are Offered: Summer, Fall, Spring, Winter	

→ PROGRAM OVERVIEW

Get real. You've been sitting in a classroom— now get out and get some real hands-on experience. Participate as an integral member of the Commodore team. Visit project sites. Get immersed in the organization. Interact with senior staff. Manage the flow of information from our preconstruction group to the subcontractor community. Produce quantity take-offs from design drawings. Manage submittal packages. Bottom line, your work will ensure that Commodore is competitive on bid day. Interns get exposure to different areas of the organization, to a wide spectrum of construction practices and to a staff of experienced industry professionals...and to the summer cookouts and softball games.

→ PROGRAM DESCRIPTION

Commodore is a general contractor and construction management firm based in Newton, just 10 minutes from downtown Boston. We focus on the Commercial, Academic, Institutional, Life Sciences and Healthcare sectors. We're agile, we're growing, and we're fiercely focused on the needs of our clients. Our principals and project executives are actively involved in every project. They're in the field, making schedules, driving strategy and delivering on our mission to make the construction process easy for our clients and the outcome excellence in execution.

As an intern at Commodore, your job will be to keep us competitive on bid day. You'll function as an integral member of our team, managing the flow of information from our preconstruction group to the subcontractor community. You'll produce quantity take-offs from design drawings, manage submittal packages and get exposure to a wide spectrum of construction operations, including estimating and accounting. You'll get a laptop while you're here and an invitation to play on the Commodore softball team.

→ PROGRAM UNIQUENESS

Our interns receive a complete orientation to Commodore. They are fully immersed in the organization throughout their tenure, attending company meetings, events and interacting with senior management. Commodore maintains an open culture, based on performance, leadership and learning. Our culture defines who we are and differentiates us in the industry. Interns receive constant feedback on their performance, along with a myriad of opportunities for growth.

But the perks don't stop there. We place a strong emphasis on mentoring. As an intern's ability increases, so will their responsibilities. The focus we place on service – service to clients, the community and to the personal growth of our staff – is paying off. Last year, Commodore was named to the Inc. 500 list of fastest growing privately-held companies. We also joined a group of distinguished Boston businesses as a member of the Junior Achievement Hall of Fame. This year, we received the Boston Business Journal's Pacesetter award and made the Boston Globe's list of the 100 Best Places to Work. We hire ambitious, smart people who get things done. If you fit that description and have a passion for construction, we'll match it with a dynamic, hands-on experience that could lead to a permanent position after graduation, as it has for some of our best interns.

→ IDEAL CANDIDATE/ APPLICATION PROCESS

It takes brains, ambition and a passion for construction to be chosen as an intern at Commodore. It also takes having your own car and the ability to be able to adapt and respond with urgency to changing circumstances. Every day is different. You need to be flexible and willing to do whatever it takes to get the job done. These are qualities we look for in all our people.

Contact Information:

Address:
80 Bridge Street
Newton, MA 02458

E-Mail Address:
ssundquist@commodorebuilders.com

Phone Number:
617.614.3500

Website Address:
www.Commodorebuilders.com

CONSOLIDATED EDISON OF NEW YORK

A dynamic, engaging, and energizing experience rooted in challenging growth opportunities.

Industry:

Energy/Utilities

State(s) in Which Internships are Offered:

New York

Monetary Compensation:

Yes

Compensation Structure for Internship Program:
College students seeking summer internships are paid weekly at an hourly rate based on their degree and college standing as noted:

Degree:
Engineering
Computer Science
Accounting, Finance & Economics
Business Administration
Marketing

College Standing:
College Graduates going to Graduate School
• College Students (completed 3 years)
• College Students (completed 2 years)
• College Students (completed 1 year)

Intern Benefits:
None

Semesters that Internships are Offered:
Summer

Application Deadlines:
Individuals interested in applying must send a resume as an e-mail attachment to summerinterns@coned.com by mid-February. Be sure that the resume lists the applicant's major, cumulative grade point average, and expected date of graduation.

→ PROGRAM OVERVIEW

Con Edison's Summer Intern Program provides college students with work experiences that help them connect textbook knowledge with real-world settings and gain an understanding of the way we work at Con Edison. Summer interns are given an opportunity to develop their technical skills and business knowledge as well as enhance their decision making, communication, and leadership skills. Con Edison identifies students who demonstrate high energy, intellect, and a genuine thirst for learning and who, upon graduation from college, may qualify as candidates for the company's Growth Opportunities for Leadership Development (GOLD) Program.

The GOLD Program introduces recent college graduates to the changing world of the utility industry in a unique environment that encourages critical thinking, initiative, and open communication. Bright and ambitious students are recruited from a diverse pool of schools to begin an 18-month leadership journey at Con Edison. During their journey, these "Management Associates" are challenged to expand their technical knowledge, while cultivating a leadership style that will allow them to lead our company into the future.

Management Associates are provided practical work experience in several major organizations of the company in order to gain a comprehensive understanding of our core business and the services that we provide to our customers. During their time on the program, they are challenged to become familiar with the "wires and pipes" aspects of Con Edison's operations, as well as obtain a practical understanding of how those operations contribute to the bottom line and the interests of our shareholders.

Upon completion of the program, Management Associates are offered job opportunities throughout the corporation that align with their technical skills, leadership potential, and career interests.

→ PROGRAM DESCRIPTION

Summer interns are afforded the opportunity to work in various organizations to experience the world of work, learn about our core business, develop effective work-related skill sets, and demonstrate the ability to deliver quality work products and customer service. They can explore career interests, network, make contacts in their field of study, and apply classroom learning in the workplace.

Interns work with more than 14,000 employees throughout the corporation to support projects, programs, and initiatives in order to provide electric service in New York City and most of Westchester County, natural gas service in Manhattan, the Bronx, and parts of Queens and Westchester, and steam service in Manhattan from the Battery to 96th street.

→ PROGRAM UNIQUENESS

Summer interns get an opportunity to experience the world of work while working on projects and initiatives that not only add value, but are aligned with our corporate strategy and goals. Our program seeks to cultivate the next generation of employees by developing technical and leadership skills, valuing fresh ideas and perspectives, and observing potential employees at work. On-boarding activities are designed to help the summer interns acclimate to the world of work and create an environment that fosters commitment and engagement.

→ IDEAL CANDIDATE

Applicants must be full-time students in a four-year college program (with at least upper sophomore status), have a cumulative grade point average of 3.0 or greater, and be involved in the study of engineering, environmental science, computer science, or business-related disciplines, such as accounting or finance. The ideal candidate will also possess the following:

Skills
- Decision-making ability
- Communication skills
- Customer focus
- Technical Knowledge
- Leadership

Traits
- Flexibility
- Initiative
- Responsibility
- Integrity
- Energy

→ APPLICATION PROCESS

Applicants must submit a resume on or before the deadline. Recruitment will screen the resumes and schedule candidates for a behavioral-based interview during winter break (February, March, or April). Job offers are extended within 3-4 weeks after the interview.

Contact Information:

Address:
4 Irving Place
New York, NY 10003

E-Mail Address:
summerinterns@coned.com

Phone Number:
212.460.4920

Website Address:
www.coned.com

CYTORI THERAPEUTICS, INC.

A satisfying learning experience that is beneficial to your future.

Industry: Biotechnology	
State(s) in Which Internships are Offered: California	
Monetary Compensation: Yes	
Compensation Structure for Internship Program: Between $12 and $15 per hour	
Intern Benefits: We offer flexible hours ranging from 10-20 hours/week, with full-time positions available during the summer.	
Semesters that Internships are Offered: Summer, Fall, Spring, Winter	
Application Deadlines: Deadlines for application align with the college schedule when receiving college credit. When positions are available, applications should be received at least one month in advance of anticipated start date.	

→ PROGRAM OVERVIEW

You can gain more than just practical experience from your internship. As members of the Cytori Research and Development team, interns are given the chance to gain valuable hands-on lab experience. Our internships offer an opportunity to learn from qualified individuals in order to gain actual know-how. Imagine participating in research that will potentially help many people. You could contribute to making a difference in someone's life and start moving yourself toward a great career. Isn't that what an internship should be about?

→ PROGRAM DESCRIPTION

Cytori Therapeutics, Inc. is a San Diego based Biotech company located in the heart of La Jolla. Our goal is to help patients by providing the medical community with innovative technologies to practice regenerative medicine. Cytori is committed to providing an effective therapy for unmet medical needs including heart disease, stroke, spinal disc disease and cosmetic and reconstructive surgery. To reach its goal, Cytori has developed its innovative Celution® Technology to separate and concentrate a patient's own adipose-derived, adult stem and regenerative cells (ADRCs) for delivery back to the same patient in a single surgical procedure.

Cytori strives to build an organization that encourages the professional and personal development of our employees. It is their motivation, drive, knowledge and expertise that supports our ultimate goal of positively affecting the health of patients throughout the world. Our interns are immersed into Research and Development projects and challenges that are real priorities for Cytori. They will be exposed to the facets of industrial R&D, including regulatory, quality, marketing, and clinical. Our interns have the opportunity to learn directly from the individuals around them as they contribute to Cytori's current projects, both individually and as part of a team. Ultimately, because of the speed that Cytori moves, interns will have the opportunity to see how their efforts and contributions are integrated into our actual products. At Cytori, we seek to create a workplace culture in which our employees are respected and valued. Interns become part of our team and work together with other employees to learn the responsibilities required to be part of a Biotech company. Our work is challenging, fast-paced, innovative and exciting. We aim to recruit and retain the best people for our business, and we invite you to submit your resume today!

→ PROGRAM UNIQUENESS

We offer flexible hours ranging from 10-20 hours/week with full-time positions available during the summer. Interns at Cytori have very flexible schedules which allow them to gain experience during the school year and summer. We offer paid internships and amazing networking opportunities within the company. The wonderful group at Cytori treats our interns as part of the team and assists them with a head start toward their futures.

→ IDEAL CANDIDATE

Candidate requirements include:

❖ Expected B.S. degree in Biology, Biochemistry, or Biomedical, Mechanical, Electrical, or Industrial Engineering

❖ One year of science lab or machine shop/engineering lab experience preferred

❖ Experience with Word & Excel, Statistical Analysis, and, for engineering students, Pro E / AutoCAD / Solidworks

❖ Interest in gaining experience in a laboratory

❖ Energy and passion!

❖ Dedication and responsibility!

→ APPLICATION PROCESS

Interested individuals should send their resumes by email. Once their resumes are reviewed, eligible applicants will be contacted for an interview with members of the team they will be working with. Applicants will be given further information after the interview.

Contact Information:

Address:
3020 Callan Road
San Diego, CA 92121

E-Mail Address:
jobs@cytoritx.com

Phone Number:
858.458.0900

Website Address:
www.cytoritx.com

DAKTRONICS

Unparalleled access to real-life experiences with a worldwide industry leader.

Industry:	
Electronics	
State(s) in Which Internships are Offered:	
South Dakota	
Monetary Compensation:	
Yes	
Compensation Structure for Internship Program:	
$9-$13 per hour	
Intern Benefits: `•FREE•`	
• Partial Housing Assistance	
• Uniform Stipend	
• Tuition Reimbursement	
• Scholarship Opportunities	
Semesters that Internships are Offered:	
Summer, Fall, Spring, Winter	
Application Deadlines:	
No deadlines	

→ PROGRAM OVERVIEW

Internships have generally gotten a bad rap, often viewed as synonymous with involuntary servitude. For the record, I didn't have to fetch any coffee or spend my days standing in front of the copy machine. What I did do was put the theories I learned in college to use for practical applications. Daktronics has developed a very structured internship program to help students get the most out of their time. Anyone looking for an internship, either for course credit or real-world experience, I highly recommend checking out what Daktronics has to offer.
- Zach Pitts, Daktronics' first technical writing intern

→ PROGRAM DESCRIPTION

Forty years ago, Drs. Al Kurtenbach and Duane Sander took the bold step of starting an engineering company, with no products or markets, but with a belief that if they planted the seed of a company and infused talent, commitment, and hard work, something good would come of it. Forty years later, Daktronics is a worldwide company with our corporate headquarters in Brookings, S.D. We have sales and service offices across the Unites States and international offices in Australia, Canada, China, France, Germany, the United Arab Emirates and the UK. The Daktronics team includes more than 3,500 people in sales, marketing, service, engineering, manufacturing and administration with all of these areas working together to make the finished product.

Daktronics offers a variety of internship positions ranging from engineering to sales. The type of work interns complete is dependent on the internship. A mechanical design intern might use ProE or AutoCAD while designing parts for a display or helping with a drawing, while a hardware design intern might work with an oscilloscope measuring waveforms on new equipment Daktronics is testing for future products. Sales interns might assist with a product demonstration, follow up on leads from a tradeshow, or have the opportunity to work the booth at a convention.

Regardless of what internship a student is pursuing, interns complete an orientation, are introduced to policies and the different business units, and participate in hands-on product training. At the completion of orientation, interns can expect to spend time on our manufacturing floor learning how our products are assembled and gaining valuable knowledge on how our products work. Interns are given several requirements to complete during the internship. They participate in luncheons, attend Toastmaster's meetings, and give presentations of their experiences to supervisors and upper-level company managers upon completion.

Interns can expect to network with many employees across all lines and levels of business at Daktronics. Because of our long history of working with students, supervisors feel comfortable working with and mentoring interns. They understand the value interns can bring to the organization and offer responsibility, providing the intern with meaningful work. Our internships play a vital role in the pipeline for full-time hires.

→ PROGRAM UNIQUENESS

Daktronics' internship is a 7-month commitment to yourself, your education and your career. Our intern's complete "real" projects in tandem with full-time professionals in their career field. They can boast playing a hand in the completion of large projects such as the engineering of the displays used in the Olympics and working with high-profile customers such as the Minnesota Twins by sharing sales, service and engineering expertise. If you are asking yourself, "what will this education look like as a full-time career?" then we have the answer!

→ IDEAL CANDIDATE

Applicants must be at least a Junior in academic status and possess a valid driver's license. Sales internship candidates must be 21 years of age (other internships do not carry this same requirement.) Daktronics prefers a GPA of 3.0 and above. Applicants must be able to lift 45 pounds.

→ APPLICATION PROCESS

Applicants will need to apply online through the Daktronics website.

Resumes and unofficial transcripts are required.

Additionally, we conduct motor vehicle record checks and/or background checks dependent upon position's responsibilities. The interview process is two rounds, one phone interview and one in-person interview.

Contact Information

Address:
201 Daktronics Drive
Brookings, SD 57008

E-Mail Address:
recruiter@daktronics.com

Phone Number:
800.843.5843

Website Address:
www.daktronics.com

DEAN DORTON FORD, PSC

Real World Training for the Future CPA.

Industry: Accounting	
State(s) in Which Internships are Offered: Kentucky	
Monetary Compensation: Yes	
Compensation Structure for Internship Program: Between $15-$17 per hour plus overtime.	
Intern Benefits: • Free parking	•FREE•
Semesters that Internships are Offered: Spring	
Application Deadlines: Must apply by September 20th.	

→ **PROGRAM OVERVIEW**

Begin your career at Dean Dorton Ford, PSC! As an Intern, you will work directly with Directors and Managers and will serve in a role very similar to that of a full-time Associate Accountant. You will have the opportunity to work in many industries including equine, healthcare, construction, and more. You will provide assistance with a variety of tax engagements, and will provide assistance in other areas of the firm. We provide our staff with the tools necessary to give the highest level of client service.

→ **PROGRAM DESCRIPTION**

Dean Dorton Ford, PSC is a public accounting firm with offices located in Lexington and Louisville, KY. Each Busy Season (January 2 – April 15) we offer approximately 6-8 internships to accounting students interested in becoming CPAs and working for public accounting firms. Our interns are trained in the same way as our full-time staff and in essence are serving in a role very similar to that of a full-time employee. Under the general direction of the Shareholder/Career Counselor within the firm and the supervision of each responsible party on a particular job, the student performing an Internship at Dean Dorton Ford, PSC provides assistance with a wide variety of tax jobs, and provides general assistance in other areas of the firm with the objective of developing an overall understanding of the functions of a public accounting firm.

As an intern they will perform the following: Assist in the preparation of tax returns for a variety of individual and business clients, including limited contact with clients as the need arises; perform research projects regarding a variety of issues in taxation; attend team and industry group meetings to gain sector-specific knowledge and share experience with other professionals; assist with newsletter articles for the firm newsletter; supplement administrative staff with tasks as needed by the firm during particularly busy times or times when staff is unavailable. These tasks may include, but are not necessary limited to, work in: file room, document processing (typing, copying, assembling), reception, library materials, or the mailroom. Interns are expected to perform other tasks as assigned. Our internship program provides interns with the opportunity to work on real projects, apply their education, and gives them a realistic view of a career in public accounting. Our internship program has been very successful and has resulted in many full-time hires (we offered positions to 5 of the 6 interns we had in our 2008 internship class).

→ **PROGRAM UNIQUENESS**

Our internship program is unique in that it provides students with an opportunity to work in a public accounting firm doing actual accounting/tax work (very little menial work, if any). They do the same type of work as our full-time, entry-level hires, and they are provided with an excellent training program and access to a full-time trainer at any point during their internship.

→ IDEAL CANDIDATE

Candidates must be Juniors or Seniors, have a 3.0 GPA, and have the ability to work as part of a team, yet function well with independent responsibilities. They must be highly motivated and interested in taking the initiative for their personal growth and development, be able to prioritize and multi-task, and do what is necessary to get the job done. Candidates should have strong written and oral communication skills.

→ APPLICATION PROCESS

Students will be asked to prepare a resume and cover letter and attach a copy of their transcripts. We conduct 30-minute interviews with the candidates and make offers within 2 weeks following the last interview.

Contact Person: Recruiting
Address: 106 West Vine St.   Suite 600   Lexington, KY 40507
E-Mail Address: recruiting@ddfky.com
Phone Number: 859.255.2341
Website Address: www.ddfky.com

DUKE ENERGY

An internship at Duke Energy is a chance to make a difference in the world and a more GREEN place to live.

Industry:

Energy/Utilities

State(s) in Which Internships are Offered:

Indiana, Kentucky, North Carolina, Ohio, South Carolina

Monetary Compensation:

Yes

Compensation Structure for Internship Program:
Pay rates for Interns range as follows and depend on level in school (for instance freshman, sophomore, junior, senior, graduate level) and Discipline or Degree program:

Undergraduate: $13.07/hr - $20.73/hr
Graduate: $17.43/hr - $29.15/hr
Special Programs: Up to $40.00/hr

Intern Benefits:

- Complete housing assistance
- Free parking
- 3 Personal Days
- Paid Duke Holidays
- 401K ($1 for $1 match up to 6%)
- Eligibility to Accrue Sick Time
- Discounts at local Gyms/Fitness Centers
- *Corporate Housing
(*Available for most of the Internships)

Semesters that Internships are Offered:
Summer, Fall, Spring, Winter

Application Deadlines:
None

→ PROGRAM OVERVIEW
At Duke Energy, we make people's lives better by providing gas and electric services in a sustainable way. This requires us to constantly look for ways to improve, grow, and reduce our impact on the environment. This means opportunities for you to launch a rewarding and stimulating career. To increase our investment in renewable energy and national efforts to reduce carbon emissions, Duke Energy is investing in solar installation projects and wind power generation strategies. There will be many opportunities for significant participation in major projects as an intern so that we can bring additional renewable power to our customers.

→ PROGRAM DESCRIPTION
Headquartered in Charlotte, N.C., Duke Energy Corporation is one of the largest electric power holding companies in the United States. A Fortune 500 company, Duke Energy is listed on the New York Stock Exchange under the symbol DUK. Duke Energy has internships for engineering, IT, accounting and MBA students. As an intern, you will be challenged with assignments that are related to your degree program or discipline. Depending on the area you come into, you may be working at a nuclear site, a downtown Charlotte or Cincinnati location, or one of our many plants or substations. By the end of your experience as an intern at Duke Energy, you will be functioning like a full-time entry level employee. Some projects that interns have completed in the past are: various engineering project work during the Plant Outages at one of our three Nuclear Plants, researching and making recommendations for Compensation Guidelines vs. Market Trends, Engineering Design work related to redesigning downtown Power Grids, System Update Projects and New Software Rollouts within our IT Department, as well as Recruiting and Operations Projects.

At Duke Energy, our interns and our Intern Program are highly visible. We provide many opportunities for interns to network with each other as well as top executives such as our chief executive officers and senior vice presidents. We provide Welcome to Duke Energy Intern & Co-op Orientations at the beginning of each summer, as well as spring, fall, and winter sessions. These orientations usually consist of a brief introduction to our company followed by workshops and a networking function where students get to meet their fellow peers. These events take place at our Charlotte, NC, Cincinnati, OH and Plainfield, IN locations. As an intern, you will also be invited to attend professional sports games (Cincinnati Reds, Cincinnati Bengals, Carolina Panthers, Indianapolis Colts, Charlotte Bobcats) as a guest of Duke Energy, and other networking and team building events. Duke Energy also supplies a SharePoint for interns and co-ops to communicate internally with each other regarding what's going on at work and around the city to make for a more enjoyable internship experience outside of work.

→ PROGRAM UNIQUENESS

While there are menial tasks involved in nearly all professions, our Internship Program is set up and designed to give students that key experience needed to ensure they are in the right program. It also gives us the opportunity to evaluate them for those key full-time entry level positions post graduation. At the end of your internship, you will be able to not only talk but elaborate on key experience gained within your field of study. You also will be able to talk about key professional experience gained within a Fortune 500 Company.

→ IDEAL CANDIDATE

To be eligible for our Internship Program, students must:

❖ Have completed one semester of school and be enrolled in the related degree program (*Typically, most of our Intern hires come from the post sophomore class as they have actually had an opportunity to get into their degree of focus...)

❖ Meet minimal GPA requirements (*Varies based on the positions and department – the minimum company wide is 2.5 or higher, but most positions require a student to be in the 2.75 – 3.0 range...)

→ APPLICATION PROCESS

Students are required to apply online at: www.duke-energy.com/careers

Contact Person: Bill Phillips

Address:
400 South Tryon Street ST07A
Charlotte, NC 28285

E-Mail Address:
JBPhillips@dukeenergy.com

Phone Number:
704.382.3558

Website Address:
www.duke-energy.com/careers

EXELON

Help power the future by bringing your energy to Exelon.

Industry: Energy/Utilities	
State(s) in Which Internships are Offered: Illinois Maryland New Jersey Pennsylvania	
Monetary Compensation: Yes	
Compensation Structure for Internship Program: The compensation structure is based on the intern's year in school as well as the degree they are working toward. The salary range is between $13.50 and $29.00 per hour.	
Intern Benefits: • Partial housing assistance • Free parking	
Semesters that Internships are Offered: Summer, Fall, Spring	
Application Deadlines: Summer Internships - Fall Fall Co-Ops - Spring Spring Co-Ops - Fall	

→ PROGRAM OVERVIEW

What if you did something to make your career soar? At Exelon, we've got a place for you. Exelon is developing sustainable energy to provide for the communities of today and planning for a brighter tomorrow. Exelon knows the future of energy is you.

→ PROGRAM DESCRIPTION

As a Chicago based Fortune 150 Company with more than $19 billion annual revenues, Exelon distributes electricity to approximately 5.4 million customers in Illinois and Pennsylvania and gas to 480,000 customers in the Philadelphia area. In addition to energy delivery, Exelon's operations include energy generation and power marketing. Exelon also has one of the industry's largest portfolios of electricity-generation capacity, with a nationwide reach and strong positions in the Midwest and Mid-Atlantic. In addition, through Exelon's 2020 initiative, we will reduce, offset, or displace more than 15 million metric tons of greenhouse gas emissions per year by 2020. Join Exelon and you can share your ideas at a forward-thinking company—the next big idea could be yours! You've just found Exelon, a place where you can truly shine.

You may have heard that Exelon was ranked one of America's "Most Admired Electric and Gas Utility" companies in *Forbes* magazine and the "Nation's leading utility and energy services company" by *BusinessWeek*. However, at Exelon we know it's not all about poles, wires, voltage, and petroleum. Exelon has been named to *Latin Business* magazine's Corporate Diversity Honor Roll for three years now, and received the American Red Cross Circle of Humanitarians Award for outstanding support of tsunami relief efforts in Indonesia. Most recently, Exelon was recognized by *Computerworld* magazine as one of the nation's "Best IT Organizations" and named one of the top ten "Best Companies for Diverse Graduates" by *Diversity Edge* magazine.

Interns at Exelon can expect meaningful projects during their time with the company. The intern program provides the opportunity to meet other interns across the company through networking and social events such as plant tours, lunch and learns with executives, and various group outings. Through these events, the interns are exposed to the many different cultures, locations and Companies that comprise Exelon.

Exelon's internship program was established to create a pipeline for future career opportunities within the company. For graduating seniors who interned with Exelon full-time, opportunities may be available.

→ PROGRAM UNIQUENESS

Exelon's internship program is unique because the company is multifaceted. It includes nuclear power plants in Illinois, Pennsylvania and New Jersey, electric generation plants in Pennsylvania, Maryland and Texas and electricity distribution markets in Northern Illinois and Philadelphia. Exelon's Power Team group trades electricity as a commodity on the New York Stock Exchange under the ticker symbol EXC

→ IDEAL CANDIDATE

Qualified applicants must be pursuing Bachelor's or Master's degree in business administration, civil engineering, chemical engineering, economics, electrical engineering, finance, fire protection engineering, math, mechanical engineering, nuclear engineering, or structural engineering. They must also possess lawful authorization to work in the U.S. (if you are offered a position, you will be required to provide proof of your identity and eligibility to work in the United States as a condition of employment) and a minimum GPA of 2.8 (cumulative) and 3.0 (major) respectively.

→ APPLICATION PROCESS

To be considered for an internship, students must visit Exelon's Career page, create a profile, and upload their resume to the internship openings.

Contact Information

Address:
10 South Dearborn
Chicago, IL 60603

E-Mail Address:
Please visit our careers page

Phone Number:
Please visit our careers page

Website Address:
www.exeloncorp.com/careers

FIRST AMERICAN REAL ESTATE INFORMATION SERVICES, INC.

Our internship program allows for learning in a fun environment.

Industry:	
Real Estate & Information Services	
State(s) in Which Internships are Offered:	
Texas	
Monetary Compensation:	
Yes	
Compensation Structure for Internship Program:	
Compensation is an hourly wage dependant on the intern's level of education and their area of expertise.	
Intern Benefits:	
Free parking, networking events, informal mentoring, real life/world work experience, leadership development and skill training, and presentation skills training	
Semesters that Internships are Offered:	
Summer	
Application Deadlines:	
Jan through April for summer internships	

→ PROGRAM OVERVIEW

First American's internship program is designed to provide diverse students with a professional and individually-designed learning experience. Applicants come from a variety of cultures and backgrounds, and move through the program under an assigned supervisor/manager. During their tenure, interns take on a variety of challenging responsibilities, attend group events, network, and have lunch with company executives. In many instances, interns are assigned to jumpstart a major project or provide energy to a high-performance team. Past interns have provided new ideas, strong values, and good work ethic to their respective teams, and became valued members of First American. Supervisors can't get enough of their interns, often developing a close working relationship that extends beyond the internship.

→ PROGRAM DESCRIPTION

Interns are sourced from local colleges and universities in North Texas based on a job description provided by the manager. As a result of the intern request, we attend job fairs and post positions on college career services sites. The internship program lasts 12 weeks over the summer months. Our interns are an ideal way to help our managers jumpstart special projects. We target students that are strong academically and enthusiastic about learning our business (real estate and information). The Office of Diversity works with the management team and the intern throughout the internship to keep them involved and connected, and provides the intern a network for professional growth.

→ PROGRAM UNIQUENESS

Our interns are valued and utilized in an exempt work setting that prepares them for careers in their area of study. In addition to challenging assignments, there are several fun teambuilding activities held for the interns. Our "young-professionals" employee business council (affinity group) provides additional leadership opportunities for the interns while on campus and assists with their summer projects.

The summer intern class of 2008 worked on the following projects:

❖ Gathering competitive intelligence to facilitate tax sales improvement

❖ Writing white papers

❖ Researching data and current information on competitors

❖ Creating country matrix criteria and indicators for international expansion

❖ Building process manuals for different departments

❖ Customizing Web Process portals

❖ Human Resources Projects

❖ Accounting Projects

BOTTOM LINE: Our internships are not about faxing, filing, copying or coffee fetching. Interns do the real work related to their field of study. They are mentored, network with executives working in the areas of their majors and they have fun, too.

A few testimonials from past interns:

"The internship program was a perfect balance of challenging tasks and exciting fun events. I enjoyed the warm welcome extended to me and the friendly and appreciative work culture helped me give my best in all of my tasks. I am thankful to First American for making this internship such a pleasurable and memorable experience for me!!" – Madhavi Kher, UT Dallas Post-Graduate, IT Intern

"Being an international student and coming from a country that is still struggling to develop a market economy, I could never imagine work-ing for one of the US Fortune 500 companies. I highly value the experience I had with First American and consider it a significant career achievement."
- Anna Kruhavets, TCU MBA Candidate, International Development Intern

→ IDEAL CANDIDATE
The ideal candidate is academically strong, and highly motivated. We look for a high GPA in their major and demonstrated leadership and responsibilities in extra curricular activities. We accept both undergraduates and graduate students as intern candidates. Each internship is unique and challenging, requiring different skill sets.

→ APPLICATION PROCESS
The application process is as follows:

1. Submission of resume via email: www.firstam.com/careers
2. Phone interview.
3. Apply through online system.
4. Formal interview.
5. Offer to hire – letter.
6. Orientation.
7. Off to work!

Contact Person: Katherine Krekeler
Address: 1 First American Way   MC 5-1   Westlake, TX 76262
E-Mail Address: MISGinterns@firstam.com
Phone Number: 817.699.1000
Website Address: www.firstam.com/careers or   www.eaglediversity.com

FLORIDA DEPARTMENT OF CHILDREN AND FAMILIES

Diverse experience gained while helping the needy and most vulnerable.

Industry: Social/Human Services	
State(s) in Which Internships are Offered: Florida	
Monetary Compensation: No	
Compensation Structure for Internship Program: N/A	
Intern Benefits: None	
Semesters that Internships are Offered: Summer, Fall, Spring	
Application Deadlines: None	

→ PROGRAM OVERVIEW
The Florida Department of Children and Families offers legal internships in both the General Counsel's office and the Children's Legal Services office.

→ PROGRAM DESCRIPTION
Interns in the General Counsel's office will gain experience in several diverse areas including Foster Care Services, Adult Protective Services, Agency Contracts, Risk Management, Mental Health and Substance Abuse, Florida's Open Government laws, and Florida Administrative law. Interns in the Children's Legal Services office will gain experience in the areas of dependency and child welfare. This would include case management and courtroom experience.

→ PROGRAM UNIQUENESS
The Department of Children and Families' intern program is unique in that it offers a wide variety of experiences while allowing interns to make a difference in the lives of the most needy and vulnerable Floridians..

→ IDEAL CANDIDATE
Candidates must have great research and writing skills. Background in social services would be good, but is not necessary.

→ APPLICATION PROCESS
Submit letter, resume and writing sample to the Department. If you are the right fit, you will be contacted for an interview.

Contact Person: John M. Jackson	
Address: 1317 Winewood Blvd. Building 2, Room 202 Tallahassee, FL 32399-0700	
E-Mail Address: john_jackson@dcf.state.fl.us	
Phone Number: 850.413.0782	
Website Address: www.dcf.state.fl.us	

**THIS PAGE
INTENTIONALLY LEFT BLANK**

FRANCISCANS FOR THE POOR

Together, dedicated people really can make a difference.

Industry:
Social/Human Services
State(s) in Which Internships are Offered: Ohio
Monetary Compensation: Yes
Compensation Structure for Internship Program: $250/week, mileage reimbursement, free room & board
Intern Benefits: Transportation stipend, Meal allowance, Free parking, Bonus at the end of the summer (depending on job performance).
Semesters that Internships are Offered: Summer: June-August
Application Deadlines: Mid February

→ PROGRAM OVERVIEW

Franciscans for the Poor offers 1-week mission trips to high school church youth groups coming to Cincinnati to do community service. They live in community (a former convent) sharing meals, chores and prayer/reflection. They do community service from 9 a.m. to 3:30 p.m, Monday through Thursday. They arrive on Sunday night and depart on Friday morning.

→ PROGRAM DESCRIPTION

The internship is for a Program Director's Assistant. This intern will live in community with the high school students and chaperones and help direct them through their discernment in service. This is a great internship for students considering social work, youth ministry or social justice as a career option. The intern will have the opportunity to lead prayer/reflection in the evening. Evening site-seeing is led by the intern. In 2008, we hosted 293 participants. Some groups consisted of 14 people and the largest group was 28 people. The intern serves as the go-to person in the early morning and after dinner. The intern can go to sites and volunteer along-side the participants. The intern is responsible for producing an end-of-the week Power Point presentation used at the closing ceremony on Friday morning. The intern assists the director in preparing the community house for incoming groups. The intern needs to be available Sunday afternoon (3:30 p.m.) until the group departs Friday morning – usually done by noon. The intern will be mentored by the Program Director and the Franciscan Sisters of the Poor – a congregation dedicated to the poor.

→ PROGRAM UNIQUENESS

To be able to touch the life of a teenager contemplating a life of service is phenomenal. To see first-hand the change in a teenager's attitude toward the poor gives one the feeling that we all can make a difference.

→ IDEAL CANDIDATE

We prefer someone who has made a mission trip or gone on an Alternative Winter Break/Spring Break serving the poor. Candidates should have a belief in God and doing the Lord's work serving the poor. Submit résumé and program director will e-mail an application.

Contact Person: Chris Lemmon
Address: C/O St. Clare Convert, 60 Compton Road Cincinnati, OH 45215
E-Mail Address: DirectorFranForThe Poor@fuse.net
Website Address: www.FranForThePoor.org

**THIS PAGE
INTENTIONALLY LEFT BLANK**

GE

Learn from some of the brightest minds in business.

Industry:
Manufacturing

State(s) in Which Internships are Offered:
All 50 states including the District of Columbia **except:** Alaska, Arkansas, Hawaii, Idaho, North Dakota, Oklahoma, Rhode Island, West Virginia, Wyoming

Monetary Compensation:
Yes

Compensation Structure for Internship Program:
Compensation for interns is between $450-$900 per week for Bachelor's degree candidates and varies by graduation year.

Intern Benefits:
• Partial housing assistance
• Complete housing assistance
• Partial relocation assistance
• Complete relocation assistance
• Free parking
• Accrued vacation time
• Opportunities to network with managers and other interns at informational sessions, career fairs, social events and recreational activities

Semesters that Internships are Offered:
Summer, Fall, Spring

Application Deadlines:
Deadlines vary by business

→ PROGRAM OVERVIEW
GE Internships and Co-ops provide you an opportunity to gain hands-on experience, network with professionals, and learn from some of the brightest minds in business.

→ PROGRAM DESCRIPTION
GE offers internships to qualified undergraduates, graduates, and MBA candidates at each of our GE Businesses. A GE internship can be just for the summer, or as long as a year. But no matter what stage you are in your education, you'll be immediately plunged into real, meaningful assignments.

Internships are available for the following programs:

❖ The Communications Leadership Development Program (CLDP) is a challenging, rotational program focused on accelerated development of top potential communications and public relations talent.

❖ The Financial Management Program (FMP) develops leadership and analytical skills through classroom training and key assignments.

❖ The Information Management Leadership Program (IMLP) develops strong technical and project management skills through coursework and meaningful assignments.

❖ The Commercial Leadership Program (CLP) offers a core curriculum that fosters the development of commercial skills and techniques that are critical to success in all GE businesses.

❖ There are also engineering and manufacturing internships and co-ops which vary by GE business.

→ PROGRAM UNIQUENESS
Besides a competitive salary, as valuable members of our team, interns and co-ops may earn the same benefits available to full-time employees. These may include: Relocation assistance or housing stipends, accrued vacation time, and opportunities to network with managers and other interns at informational sessions, career fairs, social events and recreational activities.

→ IDEAL CANDIDATE

In addition to the appropriate degree and major, there are three additional qualifications you must meet to be considered for a GE internship or co-op: You must be a full-time student enrolled in a four-year college or university. For U.S. internships, you must maintain a minimum of a 3.0 out of 4.0 overall grade point average; or for master's students, a 3.2 out of 4.0 overall grade point average. You must be authorized to work in your country full-time and without restriction during your internship.

→ APPLICATION PROCESS

Applying online for a job at GE is simple: Upload your CV (résumé) in the GE form, complete your online registration, and submit your online application. If you are identified as a good match for a current job opening, a member of the Recruiting Team will contact you to conduct an interview. The focus of the interview is to determine your qualifications, interest and availability. The most qualified candidates receive an offer from GE. Candidates will receive a written offer that details the position, salary, start date and sometimes, relocation assistance.

Contact Information:

Address:
3135 Easton Turnpike
Fairfield, CT 06828

E-Mail Address:
gerecruiting@corporate.ge.com

Website Address:
www.gecareers.com/internship

GEICO

GEICO's internship program educates, stimulates and develops future business leaders.

Industry: Insurance	
States in Which Internships are Offered: Arizona District of Columbia Georgia New York Virginia	
Monetary Compensation: Yes	
Compensation Structure for Internship Program: Interns earn between $13 and $16 per hour	
Intern Benefits: • Free Parking • Fitness Center Membership	
Semesters that Internships are Offered: Summer	
Application Deadlines: Summer - April 1	

→ PROGRAM OVERVIEW

Are you ready to gain real, hands-on business experience? Do you want to intern for a well-known, growing industry leader? There is no better place to look than GEICO's Summer Internship Program! As GEICO continues to grow, we need exceptional college students like you to ensure our continued success. This program provides you with a broad understanding of our ever-changing industry. You'll receive leadership and personal development, interact with executive management and our friendly associates, and most importantly, you'll work on special projects that help us make significant business decisions and impact our bottom line.

→ PROGRAM DESCRIPTION

In 2008, GEICO was named a "Top Intern Employer" by CollegeGrad.com! That's because during our 8-10 week paid summer internship program, you'll gain first-hand knowledge of our dynamic industry, work on real business projects, and have opportunities to network with senior management. As an intern, you'll receive mentoring to help you grow personally and professionally, and take part in several group projects. These assignments could include:

❖ Researching insurance industry trends

❖ Analyzing current business procedures

❖ Proposing new strategies for growing and retaining our business

❖ Developing marketing plans

❖ Conducting competitive analyses

At the end of each project, you will present your findings to members of our management team. Some interns will attend a two-day leadership summit at our corporate headquarters...you could even meet our CEO and other senior officers!

When the program is finished, not only will you have an understanding of what it takes to be successful in a multi-billion dollar corporation, but your project results will be seriously considered and potentially implemented. We appreciate the fresh perspectives, innovative ideas and creative solutions that our interns offer. Through this program, you will develop presentation skills, leadership abilities, interpersonal skills, and business acumen. Our interns may be considered for future full-time career opportunities in actuary, product management, underwriting, IT, sales, customer service, claims, or in one of our management development programs.

Don't just take it from us – hear what our 2008 interns had to say about GEICO!

"Hands down, this was the best corporate experience I have ever had in my life. The fact that you interact with top management and impact company decisions is unheard of in the internship world."
- Bill Pinette, Liberty University, Accounting

"This has truly been a rewarding experience. It took me out of my comfort zone and allowed me to work in a corporate environment with a growing company. I was given the opportunity to have one-on-one time with management and I met the CEO. What other internship allows you to do that? None that I have heard of!"
- Brittany Caldwell, Clark Atlanta University, Business Administration

"My internship at GEICO not only provided great experience, but it was also fun! We worked as a team to come up with viable suggestions that could be implemented by the company. I learned more through my GEICO internship than could ever be taught in a classroom."
- Catherine Pentrack, Penn State University, Marketing

→ PROGRAM UNIQUENESS
What makes GEICO's internship different?

Real Projects. Management Interaction. Mentoring Focus.

During GEICO's internship, you'll work on real projects that impact our company's multi-billion-dollar bottom line. Throughout the summer, you'll learn about our business strategies, our day-to-day operations, and just how competitive the insurance industry can be. We'll listen to your ideas and recommendations. Your proposals will be seriously considered by management for future implementation. You'll also receive mentoring from our management team and have opportunities to network with associates at all levels.

At GEICO, we're committed to providing opportunity and support for all associates, including our interns!

→ IDEAL CANDIDATE
To be eligible, candidates must:

❖ Be pursuing a Bachelor's degree and possess junior or senior status

❖ Possess a minimum overall GPA of 3.0 - 3.2 (varies by location)

❖ Be majoring or have coursework in business, mathematics, information technology or related field

❖ Possess keen analytical and problem solving skills

❖ Have effective written and verbal communication skills

→ APPLICATION PROCESS
Our summer internship program is offered at select offices and application deadlines vary by location. For specific details and to apply, go to www.geico.jobs/internships. Additionally, we require that applicants submit a resume, unofficial transcripts, and a writing sample.

Contact Person: Matt Duren

Address:
5260 Western Avenue
1CE
Chevy Chase, MD 20815

E-Mail Address:
MDuren@geico.com

Phone Number:
301.986.2388

Website Address:
www.geico.jobs/Internships

GIANT EAGLE, INC.

Challenging, real-world experience. Real impact. Real opportunity.

Industry:	
Retail/Merchandising	
States in Which Internships are Offered:	
Ohio, Pennsylvania	
Monetary Compensation:	
Yes	

Compensation Structure for Internship Program:
1st-year undergraduates: $13/hr.
2nd-year undergraduates: $14/hr.
MBA: $20 - $25/hr depending on MBA program

Intern Benefits:
• Complete housing assistance*
• Transportation stipend

*Only MBA interns are provided housing and relocation assistance.

Semesters that Internships are Offered:
Summer

Application Deadlines:
Applicants are welcome beginning with the start of their fall semester through the spring semester. Most hiring decisions are finalized by April.

→ PROGRAM OVERVIEW

At Giant Eagle, one of our goals is to hire our interns. We specifically select students who will learn, grow, and flourish in the increasing number of positions available at both store and corporate levels. We are committed to developing our interns and Team Members, continually giving them opportunities to expand and challenge their skills. This way, everyone feels that the right people are in the right positions. To this end, we offer real tools, experiences, and opportunities to learn, succeed, and contribute in meaningful ways during the program and in future career choices.

→ PROGRAM DESCRIPTION

With average tenure at organizations plummeting and "employee loyalty" taking new form, employee engagement is a top priority. But how do we engage a young, sophisticated workforce to become passionate about retail grocery? At Giant Eagle, we do what we do best: innovate.

Giant Eagle's Intern Development Program (IDP) takes retail from bagging groceries and stocking shelves to Supply Chain & Logistics Intelligence, Budgeting and Financial Analysis, and more. Running a multi-billion dollar retailer requires top talent with fresh perspectives and new ideas, and the best way for us to engage high potentials is to let them jump in and join 39,000 others in our fast, furious, exciting business. The IDP is not an internship, it's an experience.

Our first week is a full cultural immersion. For forty hours, our interns become part of the Giant Eagle family through executive coaching, teambuilding, strategy briefings, and company awareness presentations.

For the remaining nine weeks, interns join various departments in the company, including Marketing, Merchandising, Finance/Accounting, Supply Chain/Logistics, Human Resources, Operations, I.T., etc. Within each department, interns are treated with respect and professionalism and held to the same expectations as first-year professionals. Since we strive to hire our interns, many roles are open positions that they can "try-out" before they commit.

In addition to departmental responsibilities, interns are challenged with a Group Project focused on strategic initiatives currently being researched or in development. They bring fresh perspectives and tackle issues with support and without mandates. Split into diverse teams, they spend time each week researching, analyzing, brainstorming, determining ROI, and preparing formal presentations. This work culminates with the Intern Expo held each summer, where interns present their work to senior executives and business leaders.

But there's more to IDP than just work. At Giant Eagle, we recognize the needs of the interns and seek to satisfy. IDP invests in professional developmental seminars, including communication, decision-making, and others, to advance their skills. We understand the need for social connections and offer events to balance the work with fun, such as baseball games, evenings out at the theatre, volunteering together, and a competition to inspire a passion for food, the "Eagle Chef" Cook-off.

The Intern Development Program is focused on steeping young professionals in our culture and showing them the exciting world of retail grocery. At Giant Eagle, our interns get real experience, make a real impact, and get real opportunities unlike any other.

→ PROGRAM UNIQUENESS
What makes our program unique is that challenging, hands-on projects are supplemented with two additional components; developmental workshops and a group project.

The workshops help foster essential professional skills, and the group project allows interns to work in diverse teams to provide recommendations and present solutions to real company problems.

Also, interns get exposure to senior executives and key decision makers throughout the company. This opportunity to network and gain insight into our business provides an uncommon opportunity for an intern.

Finally, we hire our interns. To date, we have hired close to 40% of all interns into full-time positions.

→ IDEAL CANDIDATE
Candidates must be pursuing a 4-year degree or graduate degree from an accredited college or university. In some cases, exceptions can be made for a recent graduate. Also, candidates must maintain a minimum 3.0 GPA.

→ APPLICATION PROCESS
The application process requires a candidate to register and apply online through our Intern Development Program website:

http://internships.gianteagle.com

The selection process entails a preliminary interview, online test and multiple formal interviews with hiring managers or directors at the appropriate office (corporate, retail or distribution center). If a candidate makes it through to the formal interview round, they will fill out a comprehensive paper application on-site.

Contact Information

Address:
701 Alpha Drive
RIDC Park
Pittsburgh, PA 15238

E-Mail Address:
idp.info@gianteagle.com

Phone Number:
412.963.6200

Website Address:
www.gianteagle.com or
http://internships.gianteagle.com

GILBANE BUILDING COMPANY

Gilbane: Building more than buildings...building careers!

Industry:
Construction Management

State(s) in Which Internships are Offered:
Connecticut, Maine, Massachusetts, New Hampshire, Rhode Island, Vermont

Monetary Compensation:
Yes

Compensation Structure for Internship Program:
Pay rates range from $14 - $17 per hour, based on year in college.

Intern Benefits:
None

Semesters that Internships are Offered:
Summer, Fall, Spring, Winter

Application Deadlines:
Typically, candidates must indicate their intent to apply no less than three months before the projected start of the internship.

→ PROGRAM OVERVIEW

The day begins amidst the activity and action on a major construction site. The Gilbane Construction Intern arrives at work with a feeling of excitement and expectation, knowing that the day could bring any number of challenges. Will excavation uncover unknown obstructions that will need to be investigated? Will the steel erection proceed as scheduled? Will the engineering staff get submittals to review? Will there be a first delivery to inspect? Whatever the day holds, the Gilbane Construction Intern knows it will offer challenges to overcome, opportunities to learn about new technology, and an atmosphere of teamwork between all!

→ PROGRAM DESCRIPTION

Gilbane Building Company is one of the nation's leading Construction Management firms. The 136-year old, family-run company was founded and is headquartered in Providence, RI. The New England Region, which covers operations in all New England states, is also based out of Providence, with district offices in Glastonbury, CT, Boston, MA, and Manchester, NH. Gilbane works across many different market sectors. Interns have worked on a variety of projects including the Dunkin Donuts Center Renovations, Fenway Park Renovations, Worcester Trial Court, Pfizer Groton Campus, St. Vincent's Hospital, Mercy Hospital, and various projects in Downtown Boston and at major university campuses. Our Construction Interns are contributing members of these teams!

Intern job functions vary, but typically involve assisting the engineering and superintending teams. Specific tasks may involve taking progress photos, assisting in submittal review and processing, updating drawing sets, walking the jobsite with the superintendent, and/or working with the architect, owner, and/or subcontractors. In this dynamic setting, no two days are the same; work is done outside on the jobsite as well as on a computer in an office. Interns' first day on the jobsite involve safety and jobsite orientation, as well as an overview of the project team and their role on that team. As they gain more experience on the project, interns' roles and responsibilities will expand to allow them to leverage their strengths to help complete the project.

Throughout their internship, interns will be invited to several events hosted to allow interns to network with each other, while also getting to see other project sites. They will also be invited to various events hosted by our Affinity Peer Group, Gilbane Young Professionals. Toward the end of the internship, interns will be invited to Intern Day, which is held at the Providence, RI Corporate Headquarters. There, they participate in a presentation by Gilbane family members and Regional Management to give them a broader overview of the company. The day concludes with an interactive, project-related activity, where interns will have the opportunity to present to the Management team.

Here in New England, we do our entry-level hiring from our diverse pool of previous interns. We feel this program is very important to the development of great, new talent! This internship, therefore, becomes a platform to showcase interns' potential as a full-time employee. Since implementing these hiring practices, we have greatly increased the success rate of our entry-level employees.

→ PROGRAM UNIQUENESS

Being a Construction Intern at Gilbane Building Company does not just mean being an employee, it means joining the Gilbane family to assist in the creation and execution of a major commercial construction project! Interns will experience cutting-edge construction technology ranging from state-of-the-art building control systems to the latest in sustainable construction practices. The sense of pride and accomplishment of this experience compliments the many learning opportunities of this dynamic internship. Add to this the opportunity to turn the internship into full-time employment and you have a great opportunity.

→ IDEAL CANDIDATE

Candidates should be juniors in college or below and need to be enrolled in an accredited, degree-seeking program and in good academic standing. Preference is given to Construction Management and Civil Engineering majors, but all majors are valued and accepted.

→ APPLICATION PROCESS

Candidates should apply using Gilbane's online application process.

To do this, go to www.gilbaneco.com, select Gilbane Building Company, Careers, Apply Now!, and follow the instructions for submitting a resume. A telephone interview will follow.

Contact Information:

Address:
7 Jackson Walkway
Providence, RI 02903

E-Mail Address:
asvenningsen@gilbaneco.com

Phone Number:
401.456.5800

Website Address:
www.gilbaneco.com

GLOBAL CROSSING

Accelerate your career – Grow as we grow!

Industry: Telecommunications	
State(s) in Which Internships are Offered: Arizona, Florida, Michigan, New Jersey, New York	
Monetary Compensation: Yes	
Compensation Structure for Internship Program: We offer a paid internship program.	
Intern Benefits: None	
Semesters that Internships are Offered: Summer	
Application Deadlines: Recruiting for the summer internship program ends April 1st.	

→ PROGRAM OVERVIEW
Global Crossing offers a wide array of internship opportunities in fields such as Finance, Human Resources, Operations, Sales, Marketing, Engineering, and more.

→ PROGRAM DESCRIPTION
At Global Crossing, we're focused on the future—and that includes always searching for the most talented undergraduate and graduate students that have a passion for performance. An Internship program with Global Crossing is a great way to gain valuable experience that will give you a real edge.

Our Interns are provided the opportunity to work with talented staff on challenging projects that are important to the company. You'll be involved from day one.

We'll also take an active role in your development and listen to your ideas and suggestions. You'll be an important part of our team. In addition, you'll receive valuable coaching and have the opportunity to meet key people. You'll also be given the opportunity to provide feedback when your Internship is finished.

→ PROGRAM UNIQUENESS
We aspire to be an employer of choice for Interns. But don't just take our word for it. Hear what our Interns and managers have to say about the program:

"I would highly recommend the GC summer Internship program to my university and fellow peers."

"I felt useful and necessary."

"This Internship has given me a bigger picture of the processes in a corporate working environment, and everyone was extremely approachable when I reached out to help."

"I learned a great deal this summer and I took away a lot from this Internship."

"Our Intern added insightful thoughts to conversations, participated on team calls, and understood business case financial analysis and how to use and build excel macros for displaying relevant financial information."

"Our Intern asked meaningful questions and often paraphrased back the answers as a means of confirming her understanding of a given topic."

"Our Intern displayed a very good work ethic."

"We enjoyed participating in the GC Internship program very much. It not only benefited the work flow and efficiency in our office, but created friendships amongst the interns themselves."

→ IDEAL CANDIDATE

Please see respective internship job description/requirements. The hiring manager will hire the candidate that is the best fit for the position.

→ APPLICATION PROCESS

Please visit our Global Career Center section to view and apply to our current internships at:

http://www.globalcrossing.com/company/company_careers.aspx

You can also submit a general inquiry to interns@globalcrossing.com

Contact Information:

Address:
225 Kenneth Drive
Rochester, NY 14623

E-Mail Address:
interns@globalcrossing.com

Phone Number:
Please see website

Website Address:
http://www.globalcrossing.com/company/company_careers.aspx

GOODRICH CORPORATION

A Professional Development Program with career-building, challenging projects and leadership opportunities.

Industry: Aerospace - Design and Manufacturing	
State(s) in Which Internships are Offered: California, Ohio, Washington	
Monetary Compensation: Yes	
Compensation Structure for Internship Program: Interns and co-op students are paid an hourly rate for hours worked based on their year in school.	
Intern Benefits: • Free parking • Fitness center membership • Co-op students receive paid vacation.	
Semesters that Internships are Offered: Summer Fall Spring Winter	
Application Deadlines: Goodrich recruits year-round, but most co-op positions are filled in the fall for openings in the next calendar year.	

→ **PROGRAM OVERVIEW**

Goodrich is a world leader in the design, development and manufacturing of braking systems for over 200 aircraft. Our Engineering Co-op program rotates students through various engineering departments within Goodrich to learn all aspects of the design, test, analysis and customer support process of aircraft wheels and braking systems. Typical Engineering rotations include: Project Engineering, Design Engineering, Customer Support Engineering, Structures, Thermal, Dynamics, Test Engineering and Brake Control Systems. The Troy, OH Goodrich facility has other co-op opportunities as well in areas such as IT and Supply Chain.

→ **PROGRAM DESCRIPTION**

Goodrich's Engineering Co-op program enables students to alternate work and school terms to learn valuable engineering skills and apply coursework to their work projects. During each rotation, the Engineering Co-op student supports unique engineering assignments and responsibilities as required in the design, test and analysis of new aircraft wheel and braking systems. Each of the co-op rotations are structured around the student's skills and abilities and provide opportunities for leadership and teamwork. The goal of each rotation is to provide mission critical assignments that enable the co-op student to learn the necessary skills for that position and to help them determine their career path.

→ **PROGRAM UNIQUENESS**

Our co-op students are part of a Professional Development Group, which provides hands-on training to develop and enhance personal and professional skills and provides guidance on career development. Each student is provided a technical mentor within their team. Co-ops also participate in Peer-to-Peer training where they are paired with an experienced co-op to help them integrate into the diverse Goodrich culture. During their first rotation, co-ops will also have the opportunity to meet with upper management to better understand the organizational structure and what resources are available to them.

"*My co-op rotation at Goodrich Aircraft Wheels & Brakes has exposed me to the many essential areas of the engineering world such as R&D, the planning/testing/reporting of upcoming projects, support for customers of ongoing projects, and manufactured processing. The broad interactions have enabled me to find out what my area of interest is and have given me an opportunity to have a taste of what the real working environment will be like after college.*"
- **Amanda Deng, The Ohio State University, Aerospace Engineering, Engineering Co-op**

"*As an engineering co-op at Goodrich, I have had the opportunity to experience many different aspects of engineering. I have been involved in testing, design, reporting results, and also have had some valuable customer interface experience. Using my experience from Goodrich, I am confident that I can choose the career path that is right for me.*"
- **Kyle Todd, Wright State University, Mechanical Engineering, Engineering Co-op**

→ IDEAL CANDIDATE

Goodrich looks for mechanical, electrical, computer science or aerospace engineering students of sophomore standing or higher to support electric and hydraulic aircraft braking systems. Students with high mechanical aptitude, good problem-solving skills, and good verbal and written communication skills will excel in this cutting-edge, team-oriented environment. Students with previous co-op experience, involvement in campus engineering organizations and leadership skills are preferred.

Goodrich interviews students on-campus or on-site at Goodrich. Students are then down-selected and provided the opportunity for a plant tour.

Minimum 3.0 GPA preferred

→ APPLICATION PROCESS

Interested students apply for an interview on-campus through their Career Placement Office, or he/she can contact the Co-op Program Coordinator at Goodrich in Troy, OH.

Various internship and co-op opportunities exist throughout the company nationwide. Please visit www.goodrich.com/careers to search for all current co-op or internship opportunities.

Contact Person: Tricia Botkin

Address:
101 Waco Street
Troy, OH 45373

E-Mail Address:
tricia.botkin@goodrich.com

Phone Number:
937.440.3232

Website Address:
www.goodrich.com

HALLMARK CARDS, INC.

Live your passion. Love your work. Make a difference.

Industry: Consumer Products	
State(s) in Which Internships are Offered: Kansas Missouri	
Monetary Compensation: Yes	
Compensation Structure for Internship Program: Interns are paid a competitive hourly wage, twice a month based on major and year in school.	
Intern Benefits: • Partial relocation assistance • Free parking • Travel reimbursement to/from Kansas City • Employee discounts • On-site cafeteria • Free on-site fitness center • Two paid summer holidays: Memorial Day & 4th of July	
Semesters that Internships are Offered: Summer	
Application Deadlines: Mid-October	

→ PROGRAM OVERVIEW

Hallmark is a nearly century-old company with a strong legacy of connecting people. And we're proud of that. We are also innovators, inventors, scientists, engineers, artists and business leaders. As an employer, Hallmark always seeks people to create, design, engineer, market and deliver our products worldwide. When it comes to interns, as well as full-time employees, we need sharp, innovative, passionate, upbeat problem-solvers who love making a meaningful difference.

→ PROGRAM DESCRIPTION

Hallmark is a very diverse company with a range of opportunities for a variety of students. We design and manufacture most of our own products. We combine art and science with brilliant engineering innovations (how else can we make mechanized parts out of paper?) We get our products into the market and then into your home. We create the infrastructure and strategic plans to support a global company in a rapidly changing world. Anything you can do, you can do at Hallmark.

We offer internships at our Kansas City corporate headquarters in nine divisions: Business Services, Corporate Retail, Creative, Customer Development, Finance, Information Technology, Marketing, Human Resources and Operations. While each intern's experience is unique and varies depending on the needs of the individual business units, there are some important qualities that remain universal for all of our interns.

The twelve-week Hallmark intern program combines the benefits of a hands-on working environment with the social time students desire during the summer. Our interns experience volunteer opportunities that make a difference in the community and real work that impacts the business. Seriously, we won't waste your time with busywork and paper filing. Our interns learn about Hallmark's history and how they can help shape its future. They interact with senior managers, learn about business goals across the divisions, go on market and plant tours, work on cross-functional teams and socialize with other interns—not only ones at Hallmark, but those at other Kansas City companies. Internships conclude with a presentation to senior leaders summarizing your projects and providing recommendations.

And what's more, Kansas City is one of America's best-kept urban secrets—a big, modern, cosmopolitan metro with small-town charm, room to move, green grass, friendly people, good music, great food and lots of opportunities for fun. Those are just some of the reasons why Hallmark has remained a valuable part of the community for nearly 100 years.

→ PROGRAM UNIQUENESS
The Hallmark internship program is our primary source for entry-level full-time hires. Interns keep their continuity date if they accept a full-time position at Hallmark. This will allow for immediate full-time benefit eligibility, profit sharing, and an increase in Paid Time Off accrual. This privately-held company believes that its people are its most valuable resource—and that includes our interns. The work interns do impacts the business and is continued even when they are back at school. Participants in our program feel welcomed and valued. And that's a pretty good feeling.

→ IDEAL CANDIDATE
We look for students pursuing their bachelor's degrees in:

- Accounting/Finance
- Business
- Communications
- Computer Science/CIS
- Engineering
- Graphic Arts Technology/Print Management
- Graphic Design/Illustration
- Management
- Marketing
- Retail Merchandising
- Logistics & Supply Chain Management
- Writing & Editorial

Candidates are problem-solvers and continuous learners with excellent communication/interpersonal skills, energy and passion, high quantitative, analytical and technical skills, demonstrated leadership, initiative and innovation.

- 3.0 GPA; full time student at a 4 year university
- Junior year, Sophomores are considered for certain divisions

→ APPLICATION PROCESS
Students apply for internship opportunities in the fall at Hallmark.com/Careers. We ask applicants to upload a resume in addition to completing a profile. Unofficial transcripts are required when interviewing. Generally, we will contact the students we are considering for an interview on their college campus or by phone. Hiring decisions are usually made mid- to late-October.

Contact Information:

Address:
2501 McGee MD 112
P.O. Box 419580
Kansas City, MO 64141

Website Address:
Hallmark.com/Careers

HELIOS GLOBAL INC.

We facilitate practical experience in the security consulting industry.

Industry: Consulting - Policy	
State(s) in Which Internships are Offered: Virginia	
Monetary Compensation: Yes	
Compensation Structure for Internship Program: Interns are paid an hourly wage	
Intern Benefits: None	
Semesters that Internships are Offered: Summer, Fall, Spring, Winter	
Application Deadlines: None	

→ PROGRAM OVERVIEW

At Helios Global, interns are given an opportunity to support an organization conducting international security work for both government and private sector clients. Interns work side-by-side with experts in a variety of subjects and disciplines, and often support these experts with individual research.

→ PROGRAM DESCRIPTION

Helios Global's mission is to provide analytical products and services that focus on practical and operational application. We are a risk-analysis organization designed for our changing times. We will never support efforts that conflict with our ethics and values, and our clients can expect complete discretion and apolitical objectivity from our staff.

Our team is comprised of experienced professionals from a variety of disciplines including intelligence, journalism, terrorism & insurgency studies, and law enforcement and special operations. Our core staff members function as the hub of an international network of consultants, giving us a truly global reach.

Helios Global provides an environment where professionals from varied and eclectic disciplines and cultures can exchange ideas and explore innovative solutions to the most challenging problems facing the world today – and tomorrow.

Our approach provides decision-makers the tools to navigate today's dynamic world. Our interns have worked on projects ranging from commercial due diligence work in Sub-Saharan Africa, to sensitive work for the U.S. Government.

While much of the work is administrative, our interns are always given the opportunity to provide their own input and recommendations to our team. While we pride ourselves on our professionalism and responsiveness in a highly competitive industry, we maintain a casual work environment designed to foster creativity and innovation. Helios Global is located in Crystal City, VA – just minutes from Washington, DC.

→ PROGRAM UNIQUENESS

Helios Global provides an opportunity for promising analysts to gain experience and contacts in an occupation often accessible only to much more senior, experienced people. Our program allows interns to work on challenging projects in a casual, flexible, and collaborative work environment.

→ IDEAL CANDIDATE

Ideal candidates are actively working toward a relevant degree, are highly motivated self-starters, and can work well independently, as well as in a team environment. Interns must have their own laptop (Mac is a plus) and be proficient in all MS Office applications.

→ APPLICATION PROCESS

Please submit a resume and cover letter to: careers@heliosglobalinc.com

Contact Information:

Address:
2345 Crystal Drive
Suite 205
Arlington, VA 22202

E-Mail Address:
careers@heliosglobalinc.com

Phone Number:
703.415.0007

Website Address:
www.heliosglobal.com

HENDRICKSON

Fast paced, real life work experience with an academic purpose.

Industry: Manufacturing	
State(s) in Which Internships are Offered: Illinois Indiana Kentucky Ohio	
Monetary Compensation: Yes	
Compensation Structure for Internship Program: Hourly rate according to class standing from $13-18 plus housing allowance for those from out of town.	
Intern Benefits: • Partial housing assistance • Free parking • Paid holidays	
Semesters that Internships are Offered: Summer, Fall, Spring, Winter	
Application Deadlines: None	

→ PROGRAM OVERVIEW

Every day, millions of Hendrickson suspensions carry countless loads of freight off-road and over the highways. We are the leading supplier of truck, tractor, bus and recreational vehicle suspensions, and springs; trailer suspensions, controls, and nonintegrated axles; and truck and trailer lift axles, bumpers, and trim components. Our products support every major North American heavy-duty truck and trailer OEM, as well as manufacturers in Europe, Asia Pacific and Latin America. Hendrickson began in 1913 and continues to be a leader. We've achieved that status by providing our people with autonomy, resources, and flexibility to step-up, innovate, and take us to the height of excellence.

→ PROGRAM DESCRIPTION

One of the common misconceptions about internship programs is that interns are utilized to complete the boring and monotonous tasks that regular full-time employees do not want to do.

We beg to differ. Whether it is setting up instrumentation for the testing of products at our research and development facility or designing the layout of a new catalog, the impact of our interns is felt company-wide. We feel that the major factor for success in our program is preparation. Before a new intern sets foot inside our facilities, we are preparing their development plans. These plans outline the objectives the intern will be required to meet throughout their term by both capitalizing on their past experience and participating in any training necessary to complete their plan. The philosophy for our internship program is quite simple: preparing a meaningful work experience to satisfy the requirements of the student's curriculum while meeting company-wide objectives.

In other words, how can we best prepare students for a position within our organization? If we have not prepared the student to the level of a member of our staff, we have not accomplished our goal. Do you want to experience the closest thing to being a full-time employee? Do you want to challenge yourself? Are you seeking the chance to make a difference? If you have answered "yes" to any of these questions, you belong with Hendrickson.

→ PROGRAM UNIQUENESS

Hendrickson creates a learning experience that will last a lifetime. Students often take advantage of the opportunity to become a permanent part of the Hendrickson team. Below is a quote from an individual who decided to continue their career with Hendrickson after their time as a co-op.

"During my junior year in college, I had the opportunity to co-op at Hendrickson. Gaining hands on experience and interpersonal skills required in the workplace, but sometimes overlooked in the classroom, was invaluable. I have since grown with what I have found to be a great company."
- **Hoby Randrianasolo, Manufacturing Engineering Manager**

→ IDEAL CANDIDATE

Students seeking to participate in Hendrickson's co-op program must be enrolled as a full-time student in an accredited college or university at the time of application. They must have a GPA of at least 3.0 on a 4.0 scale. This GPA must be maintained in order to remain eligible for the program. Students must be pursuing an undergraduate degree in an applicable field of study.

→ APPLICATION PROCESS

If what you have just read sounds interesting, email a copy of your resume to: humanresources@hendrickson.com.

Along with your resume, provide current contact information and a cover letter describing what type of work (i.e. engineering, finance, marketing, etc) you are interested in and what state(s) are you open to working in. Hendrickson is an EOE. M/F/D/V

Contact Information:

Address:
Human Resources
800 S. Frontage Road
Woodridge, IL 60517

E-Mail Address:
humanresources@hendrickson-intl.com

Phone Number:
630.910.2800

Website Address:
www.hendrickson-intl.com

→ **PR**
The He
tracts y
caliber. (
expertise
resumes,
and talk w
ers, and m
peers.

→ **PROGRA**
Our interns w
areas as hom

94

THE HERITAGE FOUNDATION

Heritage's intern program trains and develops young conservative leaders.

Industry: Not-For-Profit	
State(s) in Which Internships are Offered: District of Columbia	
Monetary Compensation: Yes	
Compensation Structure for Internship Program: Interns are paid at the rate of $7 per hour	
Intern Benefits: None	
Semesters that Internships are Offered: Summer, Fall, Spring	
Application Deadlines: Summer: February 1 Fall Deadline: July 1 Spring Deadline: November 1	

PROGRAM OVERVIEW
Heritage Foundation Internship Program at-
young conservative leaders of the highest
Our interns hold real jobs, acquire policy
build marketable skills, enhance their
attend events where they can meet
with the nation's leading policy-mak-
make friends with their conservative

PROGRAM DESCRIPTION
work with Heritage experts in such
homeland security, tax and budget, communications, religion and civil society, the rule of law, and foreign affairs. Depending on the specific assignment, interns hone their research and writing skills to produce succinct work products of the type used by government decision-makers. Additionally, for young entrepreneurs interested in learning management skills, Heritage offers the opportunity to work in fundraising, donor and government relations, information systems, marketing, and online communications. In addition, our interns attend weekly briefings with top Heritage scholars and outside policy experts, participate in reading groups, attend lectures by prominent authors, and take part in internal policy discussions. Heritage provides the opportunity to meet Supreme Court Justices, Members of Congress and the administration, and distinguished visiting dignitaries.

Interns also have the opportunity to acquire more practical skills through a variety of forums. For example, an etiquette luncheon reveals which plate is your bread plate; a resume workshop helps you hone that all-important document; a writing session offers helpful tips for professional communication; and other seminars teach nuts-and-bolts networking skills such as the art of writing a sincere thank-you note.

Previous intern classes have toured the White House, the United States Capitol, the Supreme Court, the Library of Congress, the Pentagon, and Mount Vernon, as well as enjoyed the camaraderie of shared meals with fellow interns.

→ PROGRAM UNIQUENESS
The Heritage Foundation is one of the largest and most influential research and educational foundations in the United States, providing national decision-makers with information that is concise, timely, and relevant to current policy debates. Interns are an essential part of this, working together with Heritage staff to build an America where freedom, opportunity, prosperity, and civil society flourish.

→ IDEAL CANDIDATE

Applicants must be rising college juniors or older. Recent college graduates and master's-level students are encouraged to apply, as are international students who are authorized by the INS to be employed in the United States and possess a valid work visa.

→ APPLICATION PROCESS

All applications for the program must be submitted through our online form, available at www.heritage.org/internships. In addition to the online application, one must submit two letters of recommendation and a current college transcript.

Contact Information:

Address:
214 Massachusetts Ave, NE
Washington DC, 20002

E-Mail Address:
internships@heritage.org

Phone Number:
202.608.6032

Website Address:
www.heritage.org/internships

IBM

At the intersection of technology and innovation, work for the world.

Industry:
Technology - Information Systems

State(s) in Which Internships are Offered:

Arizona, California, Connecticut, Georgia, Kansas, Massachusetts, Minnesota, New York, North Carolina, Texas, Vermont, and other U.S. locations

Monetary Compensation:

Yes

Compensation Structure for Internship Program:
Compensation is based upon the number of credits completed towards the degree and increases along with the level of study. Salaries are competitive.

Intern Benefits:

- Partial housing assistance
- Partial relocation assistance
- Paid holidays during assignment period according to site procedures
- Flexible work schedules as approved by management
- Five sickness/accident days for assignments greater than 60 work days
- Eligibility for IBM Awards and Recognition program including Thanks!
- Participation in the IBM ThinkPlace - IBM's global home for innovation
- Travel and accident insurance for job related travel
- Expense reimbursement for job related expenses
- Educational offerings through IBM Global Campus
- Participation in IBM Club social activities and discounts
- Use of IBM recreational facilities located at larger sites

Semesters that Internships are Offered:

Summer, Fall, Spring

Application Deadlines:
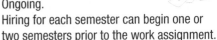
Ongoing.
Hiring for each semester can begin one or two semesters prior to the work assignment.

→ PROGRAM OVERVIEW
The IBM internship and cooperative education program spans all IBM business units and across the United States. We offer semester full-time assignments, summer assignments, combination of both a summer and semester, or even some part-time work during a semester! Students may be considered for individual assignments, Speed Teams, which are team-based projects, or the Extreme Blue™ program. Unlike other intern programs that may relegate a student to work on outdated technology, the Extreme Blue™ teams work on leading technology that helps grow a student's skills and evolve them into a more attractive candidate in the technology field. Interns in this high performance environment get to roll up their sleeves and work with "hot" technologies such as Linux, Web 2.0, Web services and Virtualization.

→ PROGRAM DESCRIPTION
What would happen if you stopped talking about what you could do in your career and started doing something at IBM?

START a first job.
START a better job.
START a change in your life.
START a change in the world.
START a job that matters.

Each of us is challenged to innovate and to push the limits of technology to help our customers win. To succeed, IBM must attract, motivate and retain the best talent in our industry. IBM is recognized as the world's largest information technology company. With operations in more than 170 countries, IBM is a world-class employer. IBM has received a number of awards for many of its employment policies. We were ranked number 11 on Fortune's World's Most Admired Companies list in 2007 and in Training Magazine's "Top 100" for our outstanding learning programs.

IBM understands the need to motivate employees with professional growth and development opportunities. IBM encourages employees to learn continuously by offering a variety of online "e-learning" courses through Learning@IBM.

→ PROGRAM UNIQUENESS

With its global scale and breadth of disciplines, IBM offers more opportunities for growth and more attractive benefits than the competition; and no one else can match IBM's unique mix of people, business knowledge and technological expertise that helps real companies solve real problems. Students will find positions in software, global technology services, consulting, and business that will connect them with real work—Work that can change the world and change their life.

→ IDEAL CANDIDATE

Candidates should be full-time students enrolled in a 4- or 5-year college or university. We are looking for interns who excel in academic achievement, leadership abilities, communication skills and ability to work in a team.

→ APPLICATION PROCESS

All applicants apply online at ibm.com/start. Through the web applications, students can view their status. IBM will contact candidates for the next steps in the process when managers select candidates for interview.

Contact Information

Address:
IBM Corporate Headquarters
New Orchard Road
Armonk, NY 10504

E-Mail Address:
mkmayo@us.ibm.com

Phone Number:
1.800.IBM.4YOU

Website Address:
www.ibm.com

INTERNATIONAL ASSOCIATION OF THE CHIEFS OF POLICE

Join a team supporting the international law enforcement community.

Industry: Not-For-Profit	
State(s) in Which Internships are Offered: Virginia	
Monetary Compensation: Yes	
Compensation Structure for Internship Program: $10 per hour	
Intern Benefits: None	
Semesters that Internships are Offered: Summer, Fall, Spring	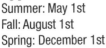
Application Deadlines: Summer: May 1st Fall: August 1st Spring: December 1st	

→ **PROGRAM OVERVIEW**

The International Association of Chiefs of Police (IACP) is the oldest and largest organization representing national and international law enforcement professionals. The IACP is a not-for-profit organization of over 22,000 members in 100 countries. Founded in 1893, the association has as its mission to lead and support the efforts of police administrators around the world in advancing the science and art of police services; to enhance cooperation among all police administrators; to bring about the best possible recruitment and training of qualified persons into the police profession. Interns work directly with IACP staff to produce and deliver products and services.

→ **PROGRAM DESCRIPTION**

Each semester, the International Association of Chiefs of Police hires a select number of students (graduate and/or undergraduate) from colleges and universities across the country. Internships last approximately 12 weeks, with room for flexibility depending on the needs or requirements of the student. Interns begin their internship on the same day due to intense 2-day orientation sessions. Most applicants are seeking credited internships; however non-credit applicants are also accepted. Student assignments vary each semester due to the programmatic demands of the eight divisions of the IACP and the project priorities in each of these divisions. Intern duties/responsibilities will also vary based on the project or manager to which the intern is assigned. Interns may be assigned to work on one priority project or a portfolio of efforts.

Administrative and law enforcement leadership topics that interns are typically involved in include: legislative initiatives, global policing, gun violence, victim response, executive mentoring, leadership, violence against women, immigration, and intelligence/terrorism. During each semester, in addition to assigned duties, interns will have the opportunity to participate in a ride-along with a selected area police department; take at least one educational field trip (for example, a working lunch/ meeting with a local law enforcement leader or a meeting on Capitol Hill); and participate in other professional development opportunities as they arise. IACP firmly believes that a successful internship program must ensure that students learn and participate fully in agency work as adjunct staff. Internships conclude with exit interviews and completed intern questionnaires.

→ PROGRAM UNIQUENESS

The International Association of Chiefs of Police gives students an enriching opportunity to gain a broader understanding of law enforcement and the justice system in the United States and internationally by focusing on emerging and critical policing issues. This intern program focuses on the areas of law enforcement policy research, policy development, and program evaluation. Interns gain a greater understanding of the programs and services the IACP provides its membership, including policy development, legislative support, management studies, training, technical assistance, program development and research.

→ IDEAL CANDIDATE

Intern Qualifications/ Expectations include:

❖ Graduate and/or undergraduate student

❖ Good writing, communication and computer skills

❖ Good interpersonal skills (ability to work and get along with fellow interns, coworkers and supervisors)

❖ Ability to work independently and collaboratively

❖ Receptive to instructions

❖ Team player
   (everyone pitches in to get the job done)

❖ Ability to be flexible and multi-task oriented

❖ Experience working in a professional/business environment

❖ Creative thinking; ability to express ideas and opinions. We value everyone's opinion and interns are considered a part of the team.

→ APPLICATION PROCESS

Each student must submit an application packet containing a cover letter explaining interest in the IACP internship, an updated resume, an unofficial copy of transcripts, a writing sample, and a letter of recommendation. Candidates will be contacted by the IACP Internship Coordinator for a brief telephone interview.

Contact Person: Eleni Trahilis
Address: 515 North Washington Street Alexandria, VA 22314
E-Mail Address: trahilis@theiacp.org
Phone Number: 703.836.6767 x392
Website Address: www.theiacp.org

INTERNATIONAL ECONOMIC DEVELOPMENT COUNCIL

Content oriented, work on real-life projects.

Industry: Not-For-Profit	
State(s) in Which Internships are Offered: District of Columbia	
Monetary Compensation: Yes	
Compensation Structure for Internship Program: $13/hr for graduate students based on 40 hrs/week for at least 10 weeks. Undergraduate interns are unpaid.	
Intern Benefits: None	
Semesters that Internships are Offered: Summer	
Application Deadlines: March 15th for summer applications. Applications for semester internships are accepted on a need-basis and advertised on our website.	

→ **PROGRAM OVERVIEW**

IEDC offers a highly competitive internship program for graduate and undergraduate students in economic development, city and regional planning, public policy and public administration. Interns work on real-life projects with IEDC staff on primarily research efforts. International development students are also encouraged to apply.

→ **PROGRAM DESCRIPTION**

IEDC offers summer and year-round internships for graduate and undergraduate students in economic development, city and regional planning, and public policy programs. Working on varied research-related projects, interns will:

❖ Gain practical work experience

❖ Become familiar with a variety of economic development programs and issues

❖ Have the opportunity to publish their work

❖ Contribute to technical assistance projects for communities throughout the U.S.

❖ Prepare reports, case studies, and presentations on economic development issues and trends

Summer internships are full-time positions and require a minimum commitment of ten weeks. Semester or year-long internship positions can be either full- or part-time, with a minimum of 20 hours per week. Graduate student internships are paid positions. Undergraduate interns are not paid. Academic credit can be arranged but must be set up by the student. All internships take place in Washington, DC. IEDC does not reimburse interns for travel and/or relocation costs.

→ **PROGRAM UNIQUENESS**

Our program is highly content-oriented with emphasis on building research capabilities for the interns. Interns also participate in a number of brown-bag lunches organized throughout the summer to learn about cutting edge economic development topics from prominent speakers and practitioners in the field. Depending on the project, interns may have a chance to get their work published as well.

→ **IDEAL CANDIDATE**

Applicants should have:

❖ Excellent writing and organizational skills

❖ Ability to work independently

❖ Familiarity with research and reporting methods

❖ General knowledge of economic development programs and issues

❖ Willingness to work in team environment

❖ Flexibility and desire to work on varying projects

→ **APPLICATION PROCESS**

Please send a cover letter stating interest and availability, detailed resume, and a brief writing sample (no more than 6 pages) via email to Swati Ghosh. Incomplete applications will not be considered. Applications are reviewed based on candidate skills and needs of the project. Selected applicants are invited for brief phone interviews.

Contact Person: Swati Ghosh
Address: 734 15th Street NW Suite 900 Washington DC, 20005
E-Mail Address: sghosh@iedconline.org
Phone Number: 202.223.7800
Website Address: www.iedconline.org

JET PROPULSION LABORATORY (JPL)

We have a whole universe of opportunities waiting for you.

Industry:
Government - Federal

State(s) in Which Internships are Offered:
California

Monetary Compensation:
Yes

Compensation Structure for Internship Program:
Undergraduate interns are paid a flat rate based on their class standing (Freshman, Sophomore, Junior, Senior) determined by the number of units completed in school.

Rates range from $450/week - $890/week based on a 40 hour week.

Graduate interns are paid based on their highest degree completed.

Intern Benefits:
• Partial housing assistance
• Partial relocation assistance
• Health insurance
• Flexible work schedule including 9/80 schedule, discounts at local business (restaurants, fitness centers), onsite wellness classes (yoga, pilates, tai chi)

Semesters that Internships are Offered:
Summer, Fall, Spring, Winter

Application Deadlines:
We do not have any application deadlines, although most of our internship opportunities for the summer will be posted starting around the January/February time frame. For co-op opportunities, we work around each school's specific application deadlines.

→ PROGRAM OVERVIEW

It's always amazing to see your ideas take off...even more so to see them land! At the Jet Propulsion Laboratory (JPL), you can see your ideas take flight. Whether you are seeking a summer internship, co-op opportunity, or part-time position during the school year, JPL offers a variety of opportunities for individuals interested in engineering, science, technology, and business. Our students work alongside and in collaboration with our scientists and engineers to regularly see the results of their work travel around Earth, to other planets, and beyond.

→ PROGRAM DESCRIPTION

JPL, a division of the California Institute of Technology, is a lead research and development center of the National Aeronautics and Space Administration (NASA). The Laboratory has a wide-ranging charter for robotic space exploration, Earth observation, astrophysical research, and technology development. JPL also manages and operates NASA's Deep Space Network, a worldwide system of antennas that communicate with spacecraft and conduct radar and radio astronomy studies.

Our Intern Program is designed to provide a meaningful assignment that applies the knowledge and fundamentals gained in the classroom to the real life situations at work. Interns work in a variety of areas across the Lab including systems and software; mechanical systems; communications, tracking, and radar; autonomous systems; instruments and science data systems; as well as a variety of business operations areas including finance; accounting; and human resources.

Many of our interns convert to full-time employment upon graduation. Interns enjoy a highly collaborative, casual environment at JPL, where working in multidisciplinary teams and walking around in shorts and sandals is the norm. Ask any of our past interns and they will say, "JPL feels like a college campus." Many also comment about the high level of responsibility they receive even as a student and how their ideas and opinions are encouraged and welcomed during meetings. They are mentored by their managers or lead engineers and they interface with industry partners, international collaborators, other internal divisions, all levels of management, and, of course, fellow interns through concurrent engineering, proposal work, group projects, and presentations. This is what keeps our interns continuously returning to JPL.

JPL is located in Pasadena, California, within the foothills of Los Angeles County. You can ride the Malibu surf in the morning, hike the Angeles National Forest in the afternoon, and in the evening enjoy all the nightlife L.A. has to offer. Our interns often get together after hours to shoot pool, play softball and beach volleyball, go rock climbing, attend sporting events and concerts, or just hang out at backyard BBQs. You'll find JPL and the Pasadena area has much to offer.

If you'd like to discover new worlds with our innovative team, we're seeking students majoring in all disciplines of engineering, science, and business with a minimum GPA of 3.0. If you share our passion, we invite you to do a little exploration of your own and explore the possibilities at JPL.

→ PROGRAM UNIQUENESS

There aren't many jobs where you arrive in the morning, pour yourself a cup of coffee, and get to be one of the first human beings in history to see new views of a distant world. Or communicate with a "co-worker" who is a robot millions of miles away. Or search for other "Earths" around other suns. At JPL, expanding the frontiers of science will be your daily work. When it comes to planning a career that will carry you beyond college, consider one that could carry your ideas out into space.

→ IDEAL CANDIDATE

Students must be at least 16 years of age and have completed their Junior year of high school. A minimum GPA of 3.0 is required. We look for students who have a passion for space exploration, enjoy challenging, cutting-edge work, and are creative and innovative. Ideal students are involved in group projects, team project competitions, and have previous internship experience.

→ APPLICATION PROCESS

Students are required to submit a resume to our positions, either through our website or their university's career center. Students should attend our Information Sessions at the various universities we visit, if possible. An official transcript will also be required. Interviews are conducted by our management either on-campus at their university followed by a phone/on-site interview, or a phone/on-site interview may be the only interview.

Contact Information:

Address:
4800 Oak Grove Drive
Pasadena, CA 91109

E-Mail Address:
staffing@jpl.nasa.gov

Phone Number:
818.354.5150

Website Address:
www.jpl.nasa.gov

JOHN DEERE

Team-oriented, project-based, developmental, real world work.

Industry:
Manufacturing

State(s) in Which Internships are Offered:
California, Georgia, Illinois, Iowa, Kansas, North Carolina, North Dakota, Tennessee, Wisconsin

Monetary Compensation:
Yes

Compensation Structure for Internship Program:
Interns are salaried, paid twice monthly

Intern Benefits: **•FREE•**
• Partial housing assistance • Complete relocation assistance • Health insurance • Tuition reimbursement • Fitness Centers discount (onsite at many locations) • 401K Service Credit

Semesters that Internships are Offered:
Summer, Fall, Spring

Application Deadlines:
We primarily recruit in the fall, filling positions for internships based on the business need. We offer the majority of our intern positions in the summer

→ PROGRAM OVERVIEW

John Deere's internship program allows interns to apply the skills and knowledge developed at school while contributing to exciting, real-world projects. We regard every intern as a potential full-time employee with strategic importance to our business. We provide hands-on experience, designed to fit your career objectives, complement your academic work and enhance your learning.

→ PROGRAM DESCRIPTION

The Internship Program is for students enrolled in major fields of study that align with full-time employment opportunities at John Deere. We primarily recruit for intern positions in Accounting/Finance, Engineering, Information Technology, Marketing and Supply Chain Management. Students may enter the program during undergraduate or graduate studies. The majority of our internship experiences are offered in the summer months, usually lasting 13 weeks.

→ PROGRAM UNIQUENESS

John Deere operates under four core values: integrity, quality, commitment and innovation. Interns are treated as full-time employees. Highly challenging and intensely collaborative, our work is constantly evolving, helping us to redefine the leading edge. As a member of our team, you'll have the opportunity to see your ideas come to life and make a significant impact on our business.

→ IDEAL CANDIDATE

We post positions on our website, and candidates can apply directly. We also recruit at over 45 universities across the U.S. by participating in career fairs and on-campus interviews. Our website gives details of candidate prerequisites, as they vary by functional area. Please visit our website for application process.

Contact Information:
Address: Use website
E-Mail Address: Use website
Phone Number: Use website
Website Address: www.deere.com/en_US/careers/college

**THIS PAGE
INTENTIONALLY LEFT BLANK**

JOHN HANCOCK

Our student programs offer a variety of challenging assignments.

Industry:
Finance/Banking -
Financial Services/Planning

State(s) in Which Internships are Offered:
Illinois
Massachusetts
New Hampshire

Monetary Compensation:
Yes

Compensation Structure for Internship Program:
In general, our compensation is based on your academic year. **For example:**

Freshmen: $14.00
Sophomore: $15.00
Junior: $16.00
Senior: $17.00

Intern Benefits:
None

Semesters that Internships are Offered:
Summer, Fall, Spring, Winter

Application Deadlines:
For summer semester (which is when most of the students are here), generally students must apply by mid-February.

However, for the Actuarial Summer Internship Program (which begins in May) the deadline is mid-October.

→ **PROGRAM OVERVIEW**

John Hancock provides talented college students an opportunity to be exposed to and learn about the company in an area where they can apply and enhance skills and knowledge through internships.

→ **PROGRAM DESCRIPTION**

As graduation date nears, you will begin your quest for that first post-grad job to help jump-start your career. You'll network and scour the internet, sending out one resume after another, all with the same goal in mind: a chance to set yourself apart from all of the other recent college grads. Your pulse starts to quicken and a bead of sweat starts to form as you ask yourself, "How am going to I set myself apart?" Suddenly, the answer comes to you. You had an internship with John Hancock, and you've got a lot that will set you apart!

John Hancock offers five unique student programs, each providing you the opportunity to get real on-the-job training and experience that will help propel your career to the next level. As an intern at John Hancock, you are encouraged to volunteer for and seek out new opportunities that will help you gain exposure to different areas of interest.

We provide challenging assignments that will build on your education and also provide you with valuable experiences to bring back to the classroom. Whether you are looking for an internship or co-op in Mutual Funds, Actuarial Sciences, Marketing, Investments, Information Systems or any of our other businesses or functional areas, John Hancock offers a wealth of opportunities.

While here you will have the opportunity to attend a variety of programs that will enable you to hear from our senior management team and expose you to other parts of our business. This is a great opportunity to build and enhance your professional network.

Additionally, we strongly encourage all of our co-ops and interns to seek out mentors and conduct informational interviews in order to learn more about the business and organization as a whole.

John Hancock prides itself in having built a strong foundation of partnering with the communities in the areas where we do business. As a student working at John Hancock, you are encouraged, along with our full-time employees, to volunteer and get involved through any of our many community relations efforts.

Within all of our programs, you will be tasked with meaningful assignments that are rewarding and prove that John Hancock truly is an employer of choice offering a wealth of opportunity. Please visit our website at www.johnhancock.com/careers to learn more about our exciting organization and the variety of assignments.

→ PROGRAM UNIQUENESS

Interns and co-ops can build a strong network; they are invited to attend a number of presentations and programs lead by our senior management. We also have a mentor component to most of our student programs, and for one program our college students also have the opportunity to mentor high schools students.

→ IDEAL CANDIDATE

While for some of our opportunities a certain level of technical expertise in necessary, we are generally looking for well-rounded students with leadership capabilities.

→ APPLICATION PROCESS

Candidates must create a profile and formally apply online at:
www.johnhancock.com/careers.

Contact Information:

Address:
200 Berkeley Street
Boston, MA 02117

E-Mail Address:
staffingus@jhancock.com

Phone Number:
617.572.4516

Website Address:
www.johnhancock.com

KPMG LLP

KPMG offers a tremendous opportunity to launch a great career.

Industry:
Accounting

State(s) in Which Internships are Offered:
All 50 states including the District of Columbia

Monetary Compensation:
Yes

Compensation Structure for Internship Program:
Interns are paid semi-monthly at a competitive market rate based on geographic location.
Average hourly wage is $24.00.

Intern Benefits:
- National Intern Training program
- Mentoring
- Networking events
- Access to the firm's diversity networks
- Real life experience working with our clients

Semesters that Internships are Offered:
Summer, Fall, Spring, Winter

Application Deadlines:
The majority of our internships are offered in the winter/spring semester and over the summer; however, some Advisory internships are offered in the fall semester as well. Application deadlines vary based on geographic region and the timing of the internship.

→ PROGRAM OVERVIEW

KPMG LLP is a great place to launch and build your career. Starting right from your intern-ship, KPMG provides award-winning training, challenging assignments and opportunities to work with terrific people and some of the largest companies in the world. KPMG LLP, the "Big Four" audit, tax and advisory firm, is the U.S. member firm of KPMG International. KPMG International's member firms have more than 130,000 professionals – including more than 7,100 partners – in over 145 countries. The U.S. firm provides internship opportunities for over 2,000 college candidates each year.

→ PROGRAM DESCRIPTION

KPMG offers internships that typically span 8-10 weeks to qualified candidates in the summer (June – August) and winter months (January – March). There are a limited number of internships in the Fall for our IT Advisory practice. Each internship session begins with a local onboarding program for each participant in the office where he/she will spend their internship. Onboarding is followed by the firm's National Intern Training (NIT) program in which all interns in the current "class" travel to a single location (such as Orlando, FL) for both technical and soft skills training. The week-long program also provides an excellent opportunity for networking and relationship-building among the interns and with KPMG professionals and instructors.

After the training is complete, interns return to their respective offices where they are assigned to client-service teams. During your internship, you will be assigned to a variety of client engagements. These experiences will help you gain a better understanding of KPMG and a career at a professional services firm. KPMG serves clients spanning a wide range of industries, including Financial Services, Information, Communications & Entertainment, Consumer Markets, Industrial Markets, Health-care and Pharmaceuticals, and Government. KPMG's clients include companies such as The American Red Cross, AT&T, Bayer Corporation, Citigroup Inc., J.Crew Group Inc., Mercedes-Benz USA, T-Mobile Corporation, and more. On the job, interns can expect to complete tasks such as: research, completing working papers, inspecting client inventories, reviewing financial transactions, checking financial records and much more.

As part of your internship you will be assigned a performance manager. Together, you'll set goals for your internship, and receive regular feedback on your progress after each client engagement. Interns can also access KPMG's Employee Career Architecture (ECA) – a web-based career planning guide that includes an interactive career path tool that helps users visualize the broad range of career opportunities available as well as the necessary training and skills development for pursuing the desired path.

Generally speaking, KPMG looks for candidates with college majors in: Accounting, Finance, Economics, Information Systems, and Business, but certain other majors may also apply. Internships are offered in nearly all of the firm's 90+ offices across the U.S.

To find out more about KPMG's office locations, visit: www.kpmgcampus.com/whereweare/

→ PROGRAM UNIQUENESS

Global Opportunities: All candidates who accept an internship offer from KPMG have the chance to apply for the Global Internship Program (GIP). GIP interns spend up to four weeks of their regular internship program living and working in a foreign country with the local KPMG engagement team on one of the firm's global clients. To date, more than 100 interns have worked in countries such as Australia, Brazil, China, England, France, Japan, South Africa and more, representing every continent except Antarctica!

→ IDEAL CANDIDATE

KPMG's internship program is designed for individuals who have three or more years of education at the time they begin their intern-

ship. In general, we look for the following skills and qualifications:

❖ Strong analytical, problem-solving and quantitative abilities

❖ Excellent written and verbal communications

❖ Ability to act autonomously while being a team player

❖ Willingness and ability to travel as needed - at times with relatively short notice

❖ Willing to work hours as needed to meet client deadlines

❖ Strong proficiency in basic PC applications (Microsoft Word, Excel, PowerPoint) with a general understanding of data analysis techniques

❖ Pursuing a Bachelor's or Master's Degree from an accredited college/university - many positions require the pursuit of an Accounting Major

→ APPLICATION PROCESS

Students interested in an internship with KPMG should contact their Career Services office on campus.

Contact Information:

Address:
3 Chestnut Ridge Road
Montvale, NJ 07645

E-Mail Address:
us-kpmguniversityrel@kpmg.com

Phone Number:
201.307.7000

Website Address:
www.kpmgcareers.com

MASS MUTUAL FINANCIAL GROUP

A hands-on learning experience that provides real-life opportunities

Industry: Finance/Banking - Financial Services/Planning	
State(s) in Which Internships are Offered: All 50 states + the District of Columbia (except Alaska, Montana, North Dakota, South Dakota, Wyoming)	
Monetary Compensation: Yes	
Compensation Structure for Internship Program: Interns are paid hourly or receive course credits. Scholarships may also be available.	
Intern Benefits: • Free parking • Tuition reimbursement	
Semesters that Internships are Offered: Summer, Fall, Spring, Winter	
Application Deadlines: Our process is open at all times throughout the school year.	

→ PROGRAM OVERVIEW

The purpose of MassMutual's College Internship Program is to identify and assess individuals in college for a potential career in the financial services industry. MassMutual's program is designed for full-time students who are juniors, seniors, or graduate students at an accredited four-year college or university. An Intern's contract term runs for up to two years. The end result should be a consideration of whether or not to contract the individual as a full-time Financial Services Representative after graduation.

→ PROGRAM DESCRIPTION

The MassMutual College Internship Program consists of an outstanding training program. It is a potentially profitable opportunity to test drive the financial services industry while still in school. This program provides a chance to learn the skill of client building and complete the sales process. In addition, it also provides students with the opportunity to learn the importance of net-working and the most effective ways to be successful at it. The program delivers a framework for developing your target markets and specialized groups. The College Interns principally come from the programs associated with entrepreneurialism and the excellence in selling areas of universities. This Internship allows students to work side-by-side with agency professionals and learn real- world business skills. The MassMutual Internship Program also provides college students with a chance to "career sample" the insurance industry from the perspective of a Financial Services Representative. This program is geared to take a student from orientation to market development to working in a mentor relationship as a Financial Services Representative. Upon completion of the College Internship Program, students will be evaluated, including a self-evaluation as to whether a career contract will be offered.

→ PROGRAM UNIQUENESS

MassMutual brings "real world" experience to the intern program. It gives students an opportunity to be in business for themselves but not by themselves.

→ IDEAL CANDIDATE

Internships are offered to juniors or seniors. Each candidate will need to provide a resume and participate in a structured interview process to determine if they qualify for the program.

→ APPLICATION PROCESS

Resume submission via:
www.massmutual.com/mycareer

Contact Person: Christopher M. Panell

Address:
1295 State Street
Springfield, MA 01111

E-Mail Address:
cpanell@massmutual.com

Phone Number:
413.744.5498

Website Address:
www.massmutual.com/mycareer

MERCK & CO., INC.

Our Work Is Someone's Hope. Join Us.

Industry:
Pharmaceutical

State(s) in Which Internships are Offered:
California, Massachusetts, New Hampshire, New Jersey, North Carolina, Pennsylvania, Virginia

Monetary Compensation:
Yes

Compensation Structure for Internship Program:
Varies based on compensation guidelines, major and year in school

Intern Benefits:
• Partial housing assistance
• Complete housing assistance
• Partial relocation assistance
• Complete relocation assistance
• Transportation stipend
• Free parking
• Daily transportation for those in subsidized housing locations
• Fitness center at some housing locations (free)

Semesters that Internships are Offered:
Summer, Fall, Spring, Winter

Application Deadlines:
Interested students must apply on-line via www.merck.com/careers/university. Application deadline for upcoming summer internships is February 15. Co-operative assignments occur throughout the year and also require on-line application via the above mentioned website.

→ **PROGRAM OVERVIEW**

You're unique, remarkable and multi-faceted. Fortunately, so are our internships. As an emerging professional, internship/co-op assignments offer an invaluable career experience. It's important to choose the right company—one that values your talents, interests and wealth of knowledge. Merck offers positions for college students at many levels, both undergraduate and graduate. Our interns/co-ops (comprised of some of the best and brightest college students) have the opportunity to showcase their many skills through projects that make a real impact. If you're the type of person who values making a difference in human health while expanding your career, explore our program.

→ **PROGRAM DESCRIPTION**

Merck & Co., Inc. is a global research-driven pharmaceutical company dedicated to putting patients first. Established in 1891, Merck discovers, develops, manufactures and markets vaccines and medicines to address unmet medical needs. Our major task of addressing unmet medical needs is supported by employees operating in approximately 140 countries. The company devotes extensive efforts to increase access to medicines through far-reaching programs that not only donate Merck medicines, but help deliver them to the people who need them. Merck also publishes unbiased health information as a not-for-profit service.

Merck offers a robust "Future Talent Program" (FTP) for interns and co-ops with opportunities for 10- to 12-week summer internships as well as 4+ month co-operative assignments. On average, Merck welcomes approximately 300 summer interns and 125 co-ops across various sites in the U. S.

The Future Talent Program is designed to provide exemplary university students with the opportunity to work on meaningful assignments and gain real-world experience. The program is strategically aligned for attracting, developing, and retaining top talent that are essential to achieve Merck's business objectives. Merck recruits individuals pursuing a wide variety of degrees including Bachelor of Science, Master's, PhD, MBA and Doctor of Veterinary Medicine, spanning across multiple disciplines. Interns and co-ops work in many divisions of our organization, including research, manufacturing, sales and marketing, public affairs, human resources, finance and computer resources. Interns and co-ops are assigned to at least one project, such as drug research using genomics, market research of cardiovascular drugs, or helping to develop the company's computer infrastructure (just to name a few). Some Merck internships include a final presentation or report. All students are evaluated by their managers and also asked to provide feedback on the program, their work assignment, as well as manager at the end of the program.

Students joining the program during the summer may be eligible to receive housing assistance and transportation to and from work. Summer participants also participate in planned learning events and social activities.

→ PROGRAM UNIQUENESS

Merck Future Talent Program assignments provide a unique outlet for increasing your knowledge and understanding of Merck and the pharmaceutical industry—from training sessions, to mentors, to opportunities to meet with members of senior management and discuss company strategy. All participants of the FTP receive a competitive salary and opportunity to develop themselves by working on meaningful assignments. By the end of your assignment, you'll have gained insight into Merck's vision, experienced our corporate culture and expanded your lifelong career potential.

→ IDEAL CANDIDATE

Eligible students must be currently enrolled in a university at time of application.

→ APPLICATION PROCESS

Applicants should visit the "University Opportunities" section of www.merck.com/careers to create a profile and search for opportunities.

Also, be sure to include any geographic preferences in your cover letter. After searching for and applying to desired opportunities, our recruiters will contact you as appropriate.

Contact Information:

Address:
Merck Headquarters
One Merck Drive
Whitehouse Station, NJ 08889-0100

Website Address:
www.merck.com/careers/university

MONDIAL ASSISTANCE

Our Internship Program gives you the tools to take the next step.

Industry:	
Insurance	
State(s) in Which Internships are Offered:	
Virginia	
Monetary Compensation:	
Yes	
Compensation Structure for Internship Program:	
$10 to $12 per hour - based on position	
Intern Benefits:	
None	
Semesters that Internships are Offered:	
Summer	
Application Deadlines:	
Intern positions will be posted every year in March. Applications must be received by May.	

→ PROGRAM OVERVIEW

Mondial Assistance offers a ten week Internship Program focused on giving students corporate work experience within an international travel insurance environment.

→ PROGRAM DESCRIPTION

Mondial Assistance is one of the world's largest providers of specialty insurance and assistance services. In the U.S., we're best known for our Access America® travel insurance and Event Ticket Protector insurance. But we also provide medical assistance to millions of health plan members traveling abroad, and concierge services to millions more credit card users.

In fact, over 100 million Americans rely on us each year, whether we're answering routine questions or helping with complex medical and travel emergencies.

Mondial Assistance is looking for the best and brightest to help perpetuate our growth. Our Internship Program allows students to complete a ten-week internship within various departments throughout the organization (includes marketing, sales, client services, actuarial services, underwriting, operations, IT and finance). Each Intern is given a project to complete throughout the ten week program. At the end of the ten weeks, Interns will present their project findings, etc, to representatives throughout the organization. The Internship Program includes one-on-one meetings with mentors within the represented department; Lunch and Learns focused on learning about various departments and methodologies (examples would be Insurance 101, Project Management, etc); and networking events throughout the organization and community.

Our US office is based in Richmond, Virginia, and is home to over 720 employees who speak 37 languages to help customers anytime, anywhere, and for virtually any reason. Our stylish, modern office adds to our international flair while also providing a comfortable workspace, which includes a casual dress code.

→ PROGRAM UNIQUENESS

Mondial Assistance's Internship Program allows students to get hands on experience working on a specific project within a department. This has allowed Interns to not only learn about the day-to-day operations within a department, but also get exposure to leading a project within a corporate environment.

→ **IDEAL CANDIDATE**

Third- and fourth-year students only.

→ **APPLICATION PROCESS**

Application process requires applying online for a position. Interview process includes an on-site interview.

Contact Person: Recruiting Team

Address:
2805 N. Parham Road
Richmond, VA 23294

E-Mail Address:
hr7@mondialusa.com

Phone Number:
804.673.1458

Website Address:
www.mondialusa.com

MS&L

MS&L offers a dynamic, educational and rewarding summer internship program.

Industry: Communications - Marketing/PR	
State(s) in Which Internships are Offered: 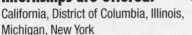 California, District of Columbia, Illinois, Michigan, New York	
Monetary Compensation: Yes	
Compensation Structure for Internship Program: Hourly rate	
Intern Benefits: None	
Semesters that Internships are Offered: Summer	
Application Deadlines: Application deadlines change from year to year. Visit the MS&L website at www.mslworldwide.com for more information.	

→ **PROGRAM OVERVIEW**

"Seated around tables in a Midtown office tower, a group of photogenic up-and-comers in business attire brainstorm concepts for selling a product. As they pitch ideas, they know their efforts are being judged and that a plum job awaits those who rise to the top. It's a familiar premise, but this isn't The Apprentice. *It's the 'Intern Challenge' at MS&L."*
- **New York Post, "The Intern" (4/30/07)**

→ **PROGRAM DESCRIPTION**

MS&L is a leading global communications firm and part of MS&L Worldwide, a network of communications brands and consultancies with 54 offices in North America, Latin America, Europe, the Middle East, Africa, and Asia, as well as an extensive affiliate network. The agency specializes in using research, insights and technology to create and execute powerful communications strategies that are critical to client success. With a unique combination of advice, advocacy and action, MS&L delivers measurable business results for many of the world's largest companies and most successful brands. MS&L is known for its talented and committed people, unparalleled client service and collegial culture.

While working at MS&L, interns will have a chance to see how the agency promotes blockbuster pharmaceutical product launches, creates breakthrough and insightful consumer marketing campaigns, keeps financial services clients on the front pages through top-tier media relations, and engages clients in digital and social media. MS&L offers summer internships in all offices around the North American network. The New York office internship program is highlighted below.

Summer interns in the New York office will gain a great foundation in the inner workings of a PR agency through the following:

Practice Group Assignments:
Interns get hands-on experience working on client service teams, including individual and team projects. They are assigned to work in a specific practice group: Healthcare, Consumer, Corporate, Media, Digital, Insights & Research, and Entertainment – and will work with some of the most accomplished veterans in public relations. Interns will have exposure to writing press releases, research, brainstorming, and creating media lists, to name a few.

Mentoring:
Interns are assigned a professional mentor from within their practice group. An experienced PR

professional is there to guide them along the way throughout the summer experience.

Team Program Development:

Over the summer, the interns will be split into two teams and be given a challenge – developing a PR program for one of MS&L's clients. They'll be supported by a team coach from among MS&L's senior managers, and will make a formal presentation.

Training:

Throughout the summer, they will attend a series of PR agency-related training classes covering a variety of topics including creative development, PR writing, media relations, client service, digital/social media, and others.

→ PROGRAM UNIQUENESS

From a pool of over 200 applicants, the top twenty-five intern candidates will be invited to the MS&L Summer Internship Challenge Day in their NY office. The chosen applicants will meet with MS&L staff and will participate in a brainstorming session, one-on-one interviews, and complete a writing/editing test. MS&L will then choose ten of these eager candidates to participate in an eight-week-long summer internship. In fact, the competition does not end there. According to Jim Tsokanos, President of MS&L North America, the internship can be thought of as "an eight-week-long job interview".

→ IDEAL CANDIDATE

Candidates must have completed their junior or senior year of undergraduate college and have an overall GPA of 3.0 or higher. Candidates must be available to visit the New York office for the Internship Challenge Day (date TBD in April) and be available to work there 5 days per week (full-time), for 8 weeks starting in June.

→ APPLICATION PROCESS

Candidates will be required to submit a resume and cover letter. They will also be required to answer a few short answer questions (which change from year to year).

Each year the application comes out in February and can be found on MS&L's website at: www.mslworldwide.com.

Contact Information:

Address:
1675 Broadway
New York, NY 10019

E-Mail Address:
NYCareers@mslworldwide.com

Phone Number:
212.468.4200

Website Address:
www.mslworldwide.com

NASA - GODDARD SPACE FLIGHT CENTER

Begin a Career at NASA/GSFC - The Sky is No Limit!

Industry:	
Government - Federal	

State(s) in Which Internships are Offered:
Maryland, Virginia, West Virginia

Monetary Compensation:
Yes

Compensation Structure for Internship Program:
Hourly compensation based on level in college.
Ranges from $14.25 – $24.15.

Intern Benefits: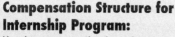
- Free Parking
- Health insurance
- Alternative Work Schedule
- Flexible hours of work
- Sick Leave
- Life Insurance
- Tuition Assistance

Semesters that Internships are Offered:
Summer, Fall, Spring, Winter

Application Deadlines:
Applications are accepted all year.

→ **PROGRAM OVERVIEW**

The Cooperative Education Program (Co-op) is an important link in the education process that integrates college-level academic study with full-time, meaningful work experience. This is achieved through a working agreement between Goddard Space Flight Center (GSFC) and a number of educational institutions. This agreement allows the students, through study and work experience, to enhance their academic knowledge, personal development, and professional preparation. Additionally, Co-op employees earn income that is based on the level of education and work experience they have attained. The Co-op Program is one of the primary sources of entry-level employment for NASA/GSFC.

→ **PROGRAM DESCRIPTION**

Goddard's role in fulfilling the NASA vision begins with scientific exploration to revolutionize knowledge of the Earth and the universe by using the unique vantage point – space – to look back at the Earth beyond its fogging atmosphere to the beginning of the birth of the universe. Our goal is to extend human understanding and to enhance life here on Earth through new knowledge and its application to commerce, education, and everyday life.

Engineering and Science Co-ops assist higher-grade scientists or engineers in technical work and research pertinent to the organization and its mission. These assignments usually involve a wide variety of detailed operations which can include planning and conducting research, development, and preparation of new specifications on similar or related types of equipment. The student will be given projects with varying degrees of difficulty depending on academic and/or work experience and interest. Candidates should be pursuing a BS, MS or PhD in Aerospace Engineering; Computer Engineering; Computer Science; Electrical/Electronic Engineering; Environmental Engineering; Mechanical Engineering; Reliability Engineering; or Physics.

Professional and Administrative Co-ops assist higher-grade specialists in support of the Center's institutional requirements. Assignments typically include researching and preparing documentation for a variety of related tasks which prepare the student to eventually become intricately involved with an overall planning and execution process. The student will be given projects with varying degrees of difficulty depending on academic and/or work experience and interest. Candidates should be pursuing their Bachelor's or MBA in: Accounting; General Business; Human Resources; Management Information Systems.

GSFC has a campus-like atmosphere where students can utilize the following services:

- Cafeterias
- Health Unit
- NASA Credit Union
- GSFC Employee Welfare Association (GEWA) Store
- GEWA Recreation Center
- Employee Assistance Program
- Fitness Facility
- Technical Library

The GEWA also sponsors over 50 clubs and Leagues including:

- Aerobic Fitness Club
- Basketball League
- Bowling League
- Karate Club
- Ski Club
- Soccer League
- Softball League
- Tennis Club
- Volleyball League
- Art Club
- Astronomy Club
- Bible Club
- Black History Club
- Dance Club
- Hispanic Heritage Club
- Music and Drama Club
- Photo Club

→ PROGRAM UNIQUENESS

NASA has a commitment to provide quality opportunities for its employees. A number of programs are designed to provide employees with the training and experience they need to develop and excel in their chosen careers. Tuition assistance is offered to undergraduate and graduate students if they maintain a 2.9 GPA and have received a work rating of "meets or exceeds expectations" or better in their latest work period. Co-ops meeting this criterion are eligible for payment of tuition, matriculation and laboratory fees up to $2,500 per semester or $1,625 per quarter per degree, with a total cap of $10,000.

→ IDEAL CANDIDATE

Applicants must have completed 30 semester hours, be a student at an accredited university, be enrolled in their school's Cooperative Education Program, be a U.S. citizen, and have a good scholastic standing (minimum 2.9 G.P.A. overall).

→ APPLICATION PROCESS

Forward a resume (to include GPA and estimated graduation date) to GSFC's Co-op coordinator, Janine Dolinka, at janine.dolinka@nasa.gov.

Contact Person: Janine Dolinka

Address:
8800 Greenbelt Rd.
B1, Room 235
Greenbelt, MD 20771

E-Mail Address:
janine.dolinka@nasa.gov

Phone Number:
301.286.9951

Website Address:
http://www.nasa.gov/centers/goddard/education/coop.html

NATIONAL INSTITUTE OF STANDARDS & TECHNOLOGY (NIST)

Undergraduates gain hands-on scientific research at a world-class government laboratory.

Industry: Government - Federal	
State(s) in Which Internships are Offered: Colorado Maryland	
Monetary Compensation: Yes	
Compensation Structure for Internship Program: $363.64 per week (or $4,000 for 11 week summer term)	
Intern Benefits: • Complete housing assistance • Transportation stipend • Free parking • Free bus available between apartment and work	
Semesters that Internships are Offered: Summer	
Application Deadlines: Summer - February 15th	

→ PROGRAM OVERVIEW

Curious about physics, electronics, manufacturing, chemistry, materials science, or structural engineering? Intrigued by nanotechnology, fire research, information technology, or robotics? Tickled by biotechnology or biometrics? Have an intellectual fancy for superconductors or, perhaps, semiconductors? Here's a chance to satisfy that curiosity.

Spend the summer working elbow-to-elbow with researchers at the National Institute of Standards and Technology, one of the world's leading research organizations and home to three Nobel Prize winners. Gain valuable hands-on experience, work with cutting-edge technology, network with students from all across the nation, sample the Washington, D.C. or Boulder, CO area, and get paid while you learn.

→ PROGRAM DESCRIPTION

From automated teller machines and atomic clocks to mammograms and semiconductors, innumerable products and services rely in some way on technology, measurement, and standards provided by the National Institute of Standards and Technology (NIST). NIST's Summer Undergraduate Research Fellowship (SURF) program gives undergraduate students a chance to gain valuable scientific research experience by working on projects of economic importance. The program, co-sponsored by the National Science Foundation, is committed to attracting and training future generations of scientists and engineers.

SURF students work on their own project for 11 weeks and contribute to an ongoing research project under the guidance of a NIST scientist or engineer from one of the Institute's nine major laboratories (Building and Fire Research, Chemical Sciences, Electronics and Electrical Engineering, Information Technology, Manufacturing Engineering, Materials Science, Neutron Research, Nanoscale Science and Technology, and Physics). A summer-long lecture series and tours expose students to a sampling of diverse research topics. Besides work, SURF has time built in for fun too.

SURF is a competitive program. Applications submitted by the student are ranked and reviewed, and students are matched with advisors based on technical interests. About 125 fellowships in Gaithersburg, MD and another 22 fellowships in Boulder, CO are awarded each year. Over 1,000 students have participated in the SURF program since 1993; when asked about their experience, 83% said SURF helped them make a decision about their career, 73% said SURF helped them make a decision about their field of study, and 94% said that SURF gave them a deeper understanding of what it is like to be a research scientist.

Just recently, a NIST Post Doctoral fellow and former SURF student commented:

"After spending the summer here, I got a real taste for what research was about. My advisor was the first person to plant the PostDoc seed in my head. Throughout my entire graduate program, I always kept NIST in the back of my head as where I could wind up when I was finished."

The SURF program regularly receives rave reviews from its participants:

"I have a much better idea of what I want to do in the future", *"...one of the most valuable experiences that I will appreciate for the rest of my life"*, *"The work I did this summer will actually make a difference in industry."*, and *"The hands on experimental experience was second to none."*

→ PROGRAM UNIQUENESS

The SURF program gives undergraduate students a chance to contribute to ongoing multi-disciplinary research projects under the guidance of a NIST scientist or engineer, and not just do busy work for the summer. Students gain valuable hands-on research experience, work with cutting-edge technology and equipment, and network with peers from across the nation. Based on their summer research, SURF students have authored papers in peer-reviewed journals, participated in conferences by presenting posters and talks, continued their research back at their home institution, and used it as basis for their graduate research.

→ IDEAL CANDIDATE

Students must be undergraduates at a U.S. university/college with a scientific major, have a G.P.A. of 3.0 or better and must be either a US citizen or a US Permanent Resident. Students with physics, material science, chemistry, mathematics, computer science, or engineering majors are always encouraged to apply. There may be research opportunities for students with other majors.

→ APPLICATION PROCESS

Applications consist of two parts:

(1) a university portion

(2) a student portion that contains college transcripts, two letters of recommendation, and an essay about technical interests.

Students will be matched with individual mentors based on skills and technical interests. Student offers begin in the March/April timeframe.

Contact Person: Anita Sweigert
Address: 100 Bureau Drive Stop 8400 Gaithersburg, MD 20899-8400
E-Mail Address: NIST_SURF_program@nist.gov
Phone Number: 301.975.4200
Website Address: www.surf.nist.gov/surf2.htm

NAVAL CRIMINAL INVESTIGATIVE SERVICE (NCIS)

The NCIS Internship Program is hands-on, beneficial and versatile.

Industry:	
Government - Federal	
State(s) in Which Internships are Offered:	
California, Connecticut, District of Columbia, Florida, Georgia, Hawaii, North Carolina, Rhode Island, Texas, Virginia, Washington	
Monetary Compensation:	
No	
Compensation Structure for Internship Program:	
N/A	
Intern Benefits:	
• Free Parking • Fitness Center Membership • Metro/Bus reimbursement	
Semesters that Internships are Offered:	
Summer, Fall, Spring	
Application Deadlines:	
Fall: February 1st Spring: June 1st Summer: October 1st	

→ PROGRAM OVERVIEW

The Naval Criminal Investigative Service (NCIS) Internship Program is a dedicated hands-on experience designed to provide education-ally-related work assignments for students in a non-pay status. Based upon their background and experience, interns are assigned to functional areas such as criminal investigations, information technologies, communications, administrative services, computer crimes, economic crimes, strategic planning, human resources, finance, criminal intelligence, and forensic sciences.

→ PROGRAM DESCRIPTION

The Naval Criminal Investigative Service (NCIS) is an elite, worldwide federal law enforcement organization staffed by civilian special agents, intelligence specialists, and numerous other professional/administrative personnel whose primary mission is to "protect and serve" the United States Navy and Marine Corps, their families, and Department of Navy (DoN) civilian employees by providing a variety of law enforcement, counter-intelligence and security functions. NCIS is committed to ensuring the operational readiness of the Navy and Marine Corps with proactive measures designed to prevent, protect and reduce the major criminal, intelligence, and terrorist threats that confront our naval forces and our nation. For more information please visit the NCIS website: www.ncis.navy.mil.

The NCIS Internship Program sets out to:

❖ Build a stronger relationship between the efforts of educators and the occupational needs of federal employers.

❖ Offer opportunities for students to become involved in early career explorations as a basis for making realistic decisions regarding their future careers.

❖ Provide exposure to the work environment as a means of encouraging students to assess their skills and abilities against tasks of real-world situations.

❖ Identify outstanding talent for future NCIS hiring requirements.

NCIS is seeking individuals who possess strong academic credentials, outstanding character, and a high degree of motivation.

In order to be considered for the Program, individuals must meet the following criteria:

❖ Be currently enrolled not less than half-time in a baccalaureate (JR/SR status) or graduate degree program* (*freshman/sophomore students may compete for specified positions in the administrative arena)

❖ Maintain a minimum 3.0 cumulative grade point average (GPA). Students who do not meet the minimum GPA may apply. However, they must submit 2 strong letters of recommendation from professors or faculty members and include a statement in their package explaining reasons for low grades/GPA.

❖ U.S. citizenship

❖ Favorable completion of criminal history checks

❖ Favorable completion of National Agency Check with Written Inquiries (NACI)

The internship is a supervised experience for a specified period of time (1-3 semesters). Assignments will not be effected for less than ten (10) weeks; in addition, total service from one individual will be limited to one academic year or the equivalent of nine calendar months within a period of two consecutive years. Service may be full-time or part-time (minimum 16 hours/week). Students may work flexible hours (generally between 7:00 a.m. and 5:30 p.m., Monday – Friday.)

→ PROGRAM UNIQUENESS

All student interns assigned to positions located within the D.C. Metropolitan area (NCIS Headquarters positions and Washington D.C. Field Office positions) will have the opportunity to attend NCIS mission briefs and field trips designed to provide a well-rounded overview of the NCIS worldwide investigative, counter-intelligence and security mission. These may include, but are not limited to:

• Cold Case Homicide Brief
• Violent Crimes Overview
• Trip to Medical Examiner's Office
• Carrier Tour • Pentagon Tour
• Intern Firearms Familiarization Range Day
• Case Management Training
• National Center for Missing & Exploited Children (NCMEC) Tour
• Group Meeting with the Director

→ IDEAL CANDIDATE

All applications will be screened to determine whether or not the minimum qualifications have been met. A qualifications review will be conducted to determine the competitive status of each applicant. The following qualification factors will be taken into consideration:

• Resume • Transcripts • Writing skills
• Recommendations • Computer skills
• Relevant work or internship experience

→ APPLICATION PROCESS

Visit the NCIS internship website for more information.

Contact Person: Jennifer Prasarn

Address:
716 Sicard St. SE, Suite 2000
Human Capital Development (Code 10D)
Washington Navy Yard, DC 20388-5380

E-Mail Address:
jennifer.prasarn@navy.mil

Phone Number:
202.433.2274

Website Address:
www.ncis.navy.mil or
http://www.ncis.navy.mil/join/internships.asp

NAVISTAR, INC.

State-of-the-art technical and professional experience.

Industry:

Transportation

State(s) in Which Internships are Offered:

Indiana

Monetary Compensation:

Yes

Compensation Structure for Internship Program:
Compensation is based on the student's class standing in the enrolled program.

Intern Benefits:

• Interns partnered with experienced technical experts.
• Interns benefit from doing real engineering work in a professional, technical environment.
• Interns partnered with mentor to learn about transportation industry.
• Interns may receive college credit with school's approval.

Semesters that Internships are Offered:

Summer, Fall, Spring, Winter

Application Deadlines:
The only deadline is for the summer intern program, which is March 1.

→ PROGRAM OVERVIEW
Our program begins at the high school level with both paid and unpaid internships. Our college program consists of summer interns, year-round student workers, and official co-ops and internships including parallel programs. Many high school graduates continue with Navistar and participate in one of our college program opportunities.

→ PROGRAM DESCRIPTION
A truly enriching experience in a professional and state-of-the-art technical environment with opportunities in the following fields:
• Engineering (Mechanical, Electrical, Structural, Computer, Ergo, Software)
• Engineering Technology (Mechanical, Design, Electrical)
• Finance/Accounting Business
• Graphic Design

Students can expect:
• Real work experience in a technical profession
• Orientation program • Plant visit
• Student Ownership (student-led brown-bag luncheons)
• Internal student networking activities
• Navistar Product Ride & Drives
• Community Networking activities
• Assignment presentations to leadership team
• Performance Evaluation/ Experience Evaluation

→ PROGRAM UNIQUENESS
Navistar's student-worker programs are linked to our development programs whereby college graduates may be hired full-time to participate in our Operations, IT, or Finance Leadership Development Programs. This 2-year opportunity includes 6-month rotations at locations around the country. Once complete, the employee and rotational supervisors select destination within the company.

→ IDEAL CANDIDATE/ APPLICATION PROCESS
Candidate prerequisites are based on the position requirements. Available positions are placed on Indiana InternNET as well as with area high school and accredited colleges.

Contact Information:
Website Address:

www.Navistar.com

**THIS PAGE
INTENTIONALLY LEFT BLANK**

NFL PLAYERS ASSOCIATION

Join the ultimate team!

Industry:
Not-For-Profit

State(s) in Which Internships are Offered:
District of Columbia

Monetary Compensation:
Yes

Compensation Structure for Internship Program:
$12 per hour

Intern Benefits:
• Transportation stipend

Semesters that Internships are Offered:
Summer, Fall, Spring, Winter

Application Deadlines:
November 1; December 15; March 1; June 1

→ PROGRAM OVERVIEW
The National Football League Players Association (NFLPA) acts as the middle-man between the league and its players. The union, along with its marketing and licensing subsidiary, NFL PLAYERS, represents more than 1,800 active players and many memorable retired players, and has been aggressive in its efforts to expand player marketing opportunities. It negotiates and assures the terms of the league's collective bargaining agreement, negotiates and monitors retirement and insurance benefits, and promotes the image of the players.

→ PROGRAM DESCRIPTION
The NFL Players Association has over 14 departments, including NFL PLAYERS, our licensing subsidiary. Please visit our website for a complete list of all departments. Our major goals include assisting colleges and universities which require or allow internships in degree preparation by providing appropriate opportunities and providing work experience to students requiring on-the-job training for graduation, and additional resources to the NFL Players Association and NFL PLAYERS. The NFL Players Association/NFL PLAYERS Intern Program is conducted on a year-round basis and positions are filled each Winter, Spring, Summer and Fall term. Each internship is no more than 90 calendar days. NFLPA/NFL PLAYERS Inc office hours are 9:00am-5:30pm Monday through Friday.

→ PROGRAM UNIQUENESS
Interns are only brought in on an as-needed basis, making each internship enriching and worthwhile. Interns could work on projects such as conducting interviews, interacting with players, assisting in planning events, helping preserve history, and much more.

→ IDEAL CANDIDATE
To be considered, prospective interns must meet the following requirements:

❖ Students must be entering their Junior or Senior year of study in an undergraduate program, graduate students or have completed their degree within the past 6 months.

❖ Candidates seeking a legal internship must be currently enrolled in law school or have received their J.D. within the past 6 months.

❖ All potential interns must submit a resume, cover letter, application, transcript, letters of recommendation and a writing sample to the Manager of Human Resources. All materials must be received for consideration.

❖ Minimum GPA of 3.0 is required.

❖ Students of all academic backgrounds are encouraged to apply. With over 14 different departments, all backgrounds are applicable.

❖ Experience with Microsoft Suite is preferred.

→ APPLICATION PROCESS

Interns are selected by the NFLPA Internship Committee after all applications have been received. Candidates are chosen based on referrals/recommendations, education, experience, and overall quality of materials.

Contact Person: Blake Rachel Velcoff
Address: 1133 20th Street, NW   Washington DC, 20036
E-Mail Address: blake.velcoff@nflplayers.com
Phone Number: 202.756.9105
Website Address: www.nflplayers.com

NC STATE GOVERNMENT INTERNSHIP PROGRAM

Long-standing program offering exciting, unique paid internships.

Industry: Government	
State(s) in Which Internships are Offered: North Carolina, Washington DC	
Monetary Compensation: Yes	
Compensation Structure for Internship Program: Summer interns earn $8.25/hour, working 40 hours/week for 10 weeks.	
Intern Benefits: None	
Semesters that Internships are Offered: Summer	
Application Deadlines: The application deadline for summer internships falls annually in mid-January. Program details are posted online by early November, including available internships and the program calendar.	

→ **PROGRAM OVERVIEW**

The prestigious and competitive North Carolina State Government Internship Program offers 100 paid summer internships within state government agencies in a wide variety of majors and fields. Opportunities are located across the state (and one in D.C.) and available to permanent North Carolina residents studying at the undergraduate or graduate level, or in law school.

→ **PROGRAM DESCRIPTION**

Opportunities are available within 29 Departments in the state government system, and include internships ranging from architecture, to human resources, to the sciences. A variety of state agencies and facilities seek interns, including state historic sites, museums, aquariums, prisons, courts and statewide offices. Participants in the N.C. State Government Internship Program complete specific internship projects that serve our State and its citizens. Summer interns also have the opportunity to participate in tours and events designed to broaden their perspective of state government. The Program hosts an annual reception at the Executive Mansion in honor of our summer interns!

Here is what some of our former interns had to say about their experience:

"This internship has given me a dose of life post-college in the career world. I feel prepared to make the transition next year."
- **N.C. Dept. of Commerce, International Trade Division intern**

"My internship cleared any doubts I had about my overall career path. This internship helped me in ways I couldn't have ever imagined."
- **N.C. Museum of Natural Sciences intern**

"This gave me phenomenal exposure...I could not have learned more in a 10-week period!"
- **N.C. Office of the Governor intern**

"I have benefited tremendously from my experience as an intern. Through my internship, I was able to jump into projects that I would otherwise not have had access to, and meet amazing professionals in my field of study."
- **N.C. Aquarium at Fort Fisher intern**

→ PROGRAM UNIQUENESS

We offer an opportunity to get your foot in the door with state government, gain real-world experience in public service, contribute to meaningful projects, boost your resume and network with professionals in your field...all while getting paid!

→ IDEAL CANDIDATE

Applicants must meet the following criteria:

❖ Permanent resident of North Carolina

❖ Currently enrolled at a college/university and continuing education in the semester following the internship.

❖ Carrying a minimum of a 2.5 GPA on a 4.0 scale.

❖ Completed high school and at least one year of college by the start of the internship in May.

❖ Have not participated in the N.C. State Government Internship Program or a paid internship with the N.C. General Assembly in the past.

→ APPLICATION PROCESS

Prospective interns submit application forms, cover letters, resumes and academic transcripts. The N.C. Internship Council selects finalists to complete phone interviews with internship site supervisors. Based on interview feedback, the Youth Advocacy & Involvement Office selects summer interns.

Contact Person: Internship Coordinator

Address:
Youth Advocacy & Involvement Office
1319 Mail Service Center
Raleigh, NC 27699-1319

E-Mail Address:
lisa.flint@doa.nc.gov

Phone Number:
919.789.5880

Website Address:
www.ncyaio.com

OSHKOSH PUBLIC MUSEUM

An immersive experience sure to open new doors.

Industry: Education/Academia	
State(s) in Which Internships are Offered: Wisconsin	
Monetary Compensation: None	
Compensation Structure for Internship Program: N/A	
Intern Benefits: • Free parking	
Semesters that Internships are Offered: Summer, Fall, Spring, Winter	
Application Deadlines: None. However, the earlier the application, the better the chances are that all internships are not filled.	

→ PROGRAM OVERVIEW

Learn how museums are moving into the 21st century by participating in an internship at the Oshkosh Public Museum. Do you know what area in the field you want to pursue? We can give you hands on experience that will look great on a resume. Not sure what you want to do in the field or even what areas exist? We will not only introduce you to what it's all about, but also teach you valuable skills. It is an exciting new era in the museum world—come be a part of making history come alive.

→ PROGRAM DESCRIPTION

The Oshkosh Public Museum is a department of the City of Oshkosh, WI. We are a social and natural history museum of medium size. Our area of focus is the watershed area of the Lake Winnebago region. We are here to educate the public about the area's history and natural resources in a compelling manner.

Each internship is personalized to fit the needs of the student, so tasks may vary. In the past, an intern worked on research for a book we are producing; another helped in the design and prep work for an exhibit; another developed a computer design program for help in laying out future exhibits; another learned a little about everything, working with a variety of different staff in all departments from the director down to the exhibit carpenter; and another developed an education program to enhance an exhibit. Many interns have been so excited about what they have learned that they have taken a second internship with us.

→ PROGRAM UNIQUENESS

Each internship is designed for the specific student. While the experience may have some hard work involved, we try to do so in a fun and relaxed manner. Teamwork is vital, and many who have not been introduced to that before can easily see how important that is in this field to succeed. We are there for the student, but admit we may not have all the answers, giving students a real chance to have their input acted upon.

→ IDEAL CANDIDATE

Making a commitment to a certain span of time and showing up (if not able to make a day, letting us know ahead of time). Assignments are determined after an interview by whatever staff involved and designed around the work schedule of that staff person.

→ APPLICATION PROCESS

Upon expression of interest, a form will be sent to be filled out by students. Upon return of the form, an interview will be coordinated. An interview will be conducted to review what university requirements you need and special areas of interest.

Contact Person: Debra G. Daubert

Address:
1331 Algoma Blvd.
Oshkosh, WI 54901

E-Mail Address:
ddaubert@ci.oshkosh.wi.us

Phone Number:
920.236.5767

Website Address:
www.oshkoshmuseum.org

PARKER HANNIFIN CORPORATION

Engineering internships at Parker CSD provide wings for soaring.

Industry: Manufacturing - Aerospace	
State(s) in Which Internships are Offered: California, Georgia, Utah	
Monetary Compensation: Yes	
Compensation Structure for Internship Program: $18-$20 per hour	
Intern Benefits: • Free parking • Paid prorated vacation and holidays • Service accrual • Performance feedback	
Semesters that Internships are Offered: Summer, Fall, Spring, Winter	
Application Deadlines: See website	

→ PROGRAM OVERVIEW

Interns at Parker CSD are responsible for work assignments on a part-time or temporary employment basis while enrolled in a university degree program. The work is significant and meaningful to the person's degree and interest. Assignments are intended to provide entry-level experience and training related to the degree discipline and in Parker business structure, operational functions, customers, and products.

There is direct supervision and mentoring to support integrated learning and results.

→ PROGRAM DESCRIPTION

Interns at Parker Control Systems Division (CSD) are encouraged to acquire knowledge of various department operations, functions, responsibilities and work flow. They will gain this knowledge by completing well-defined work assignments and actively participating in hands-on projects and/or special assignments. In this way, they learn and become proficient at systems and procedures applicable to industry work assignments in the functional area of their study.

Throughout the engagement, interns maintain communication with a team leader that includes feedback on assignments, scheduling, and program improvements. Flexibility and allowance is made for part-time status, including a chance to be involved and support significant projects, but immediate deadline work may be assigned to an experienced team member.

The culture of work is very team- and participation-oriented. There is space for individual growth and performance with the benefit of shared knowledge and collaborative effort.

Following graduation, and contingent on performance, opportunities for permanent graduate associate positions may be offered.

→ PROGRAM UNIQUENESS

The interns at Parker CSD typically live near a facility location (Irvine, CA; Ogden, UT, or Dublin, GA) and are able to flexibly balance university studies with practical experience in the workplace. They receive interesting and significant projects that are both a challenge and reward to complete.

→ IDEAL CANDIDATE

Students should be enrolled in university coursework toward a degree in Business Administration, Engineering, or a related discipline, have the ability to work effectively in a variety of administrative, technical and manufacturing assignments, and possess excellent verbal, written and interpersonal communication skills and the ability to work effectively with others and be a participative team player.

→ APPLICATION PROCESS

Students should attend a university local to a Parker CSD location. Student should submit resume with cover letter to our Human Resources department. If selected, students then interview with a team leader.

Contact Information:

Address:
14300 Alton Parkway
Irvine, CA 92618-1898

E-Mail Address:
cmoshenko@parker.com

Phone Number:
949.833.3000

Website Address:
www.parker.com

PARTNERSHIP FOR PUBLIC SERVICE

Paid DC internship for those interested in public service.

Industry: Not-For-Profit	
State(s) in Which Internships are Offered: District of Columbia	
Monetary Compensation: Yes	
Compensation Structure for Internship Program: We offer a competitive stipend to comparable fellowships.	
Intern Benefits: None	
Semesters that Internships are Offered: Summer, Fall, Spring, Winter	
Application Deadlines: Mid-March - Summer Mid-July - Fall Mid-November - Winter/Spring	

→ PROGRAM OVERVIEW

The Partnership for Public Service is seeking current students or recent graduates to join our team and contribute to our mission. Are you a student or recent graduate of an undergraduate or graduate program? Are you passionate about public service? Are you looking for an opportunity to develop your skills and gain valuable experience? Are you looking for a paid position in the heart of Washington, D.C.? Then we're interested in hearing from you!

→ PROGRAM DESCRIPTION

As we enter a new century, America faces a new set of great challenges: fighting a war against terrorism, prospering in the global economy, expanding opportunity by improving schools and health care. America has always succeeded as a result of what we do as individuals, but more important, what we do together as a nation. The Partnership for Public Service, a nonpartisan, nonprofit organization, was created because now, more than ever, we need the best and brightest to work on our behalf to address our common challenges. The Partnership is dedicated to bringing the best to our cause and building an innovative and effective government workforce to serve our country. Now is the time to focus on government's management and talent needs and usher in a new era of public service. Government faces an unprecedented brain drain as the baby boomer generation nears retirement, and insufficient interest in public service has left us with an inadequate pipeline of talent to replace these imminent losses. To achieve this mission, the Partnership:

- Helps raise awareness and improve public attitudes about government service;

- Inspires people to serve through outreach to college campuses and other key talent groups;

- Provides hands-on assistance to federal agencies from both in-house experts and private sector partners;

- Advocates for needed legislative reforms;

- Generates thought-provoking research on the workforce challenges facing the federal government.

These activities make the Partnership a catalyst for change. We are changing the federal workplace by helping transform agencies into environments where our nation's best and brightest come to build their careers. At the same time, we are changing the policies that shape our government and changing perceptions about public service. Ultimately, we are changing people's lives by helping create the vibrant, responsive government that the American people expect and these historic times demand. Through an established fellowship program – the Public Service Fellows Program – the Partnership for Public Service offers a unique opportunity for public-service minded students and graduates to gain a new appreciation and understanding of public service. Fellows contribute to many areas of the organization: in addition to regular assignments in support of his or her team, each Fellow is encouraged to take initiative on projects of particular interest to him or her. The Public Service Fellows Program is structured to enable each Fellow to significantly contribute to the Partnership's work while gaining valuable experience. Fellows are assigned to one of the Partnership's teams based on their skill and interest match. During their tenure, fellows are fully integrated within the team's projects and meetings. Fellows may also be asked to lend support on projects for other teams, as needed, and to occasionally assist with administrative duties, such as mailings, greeting visitors, and directing phone calls.

→ PROGRAM UNIQUENESS

The opportunity to work with federal agencies and private-sector partners at a first-class nonprofit.

→ IDEAL CANDIDATE

Qualifications:

- Strong commitment to public service issues

- Desire to learn about issues affecting the federal government

- Desire and ability to interact with other organizations including those in the non-profit, academic, private, media, and governmental sectors

- Excellent writing and analytical skills

- Good presentation skills

- Ability to work well in a fast-paced ever-changing environment and to work on multiple assignments in a given time frame

- Strong interpersonal skills and the ability to work as a member of a team

- Current student or recent graduate of an undergraduate or graduate program

- Proficiency in web-based research and Microsoft Office programs

→ APPLICATION PROCESS

- Questions
- Resume
- References
- Transcripts (unofficial)

Contact Information:

Address:
1100 New York Ave
Suite 1090 East
Washington DC, 20005

E-Mail Address:
fellows@ourpublicservice.org

Phone Number:
202.775.9111

Website Address:
www.ourpublicservice.org

PHILADELPHIA MUSEUM OF ART

The PMA Museum Studies Internship opens minds and doors to the wide variety of possible careers in art museums.

Industry: Arts & Entertainment	
State(s) in Which Internships are Offered: Pennsylvania	
Monetary Compensation: No	
Compensation Structure for Internship Program: N/A	
Intern Benefits: • Discount in the cafeteria and museum shops • Admittance to other museums who are members of the AAM	
Semesters that Internships are Offered: Summer	
Application Deadlines: January 30th for the following summer	

→ PROGRAM OVERVIEW

The Philadelphia Museum of Art is a leader in the training and mentoring of young museum professionals. The Museum Studies Internship Program provides interns with exposure to the inner workings of a major metropolitan museum, while fostering an awareness of museum careers through experiences not available in most academic settings.

→ PROGRAM DESCRIPTION

The Museum Studies Internship Program at the Philadelphia Museum of Art is a nine-week program offered each summer. Up to 25 interns are placed in various departments throughout the museum. These departmental placements vary somewhat from summer to summer; however, the following departments usually have interns:

- Development
- External Affairs
- Library
- Registrar
- Curatorial Departments for:
    American Art
    Conservation
    European Painting
    Arms and Armor
    Indian and Himalayan Art
    Modern and Contemporary Art
    Prints, Drawings and Photographs
    Costumes and Textiles
- Education, Marketing and Public Relations
- Rights and Reproductions.

Each intern works in his/her home department for three-and-a-half days each week. Interns participate in many ways through attending departmental staff meetings, assisting the professionals in the department and by completing individual assignments. During the remaining day-and-a-half each week, all 25 interns meet together for gallery talks by curators, tours of storage areas, private sessions with top administrators, observation sessions in the conservation labs, panel presentations by Human Resources, Publications, the Registrar, Rights and Reproductions, and attendance at an Education Fair including a presentation by the office for Accessible Programs. The intern coordinator also arranges for the intern group to visit other museums in the area and, where possible, to meet with their administrators.

→ PROGRAM UNIQUENESS

There are three principal components that make the Philadelphia Museum of Art internship program unique. The first component is the large group activities, tours, discussions with professionals, and generally, exposure to the inner and outer workings of the entire museum community. The second is the richness of experience involved in being part of a large group of interns. The group of 25 becomes a rich source for sharing information about graduate degree choices and programs, and the multitude of other experiences each intern has had. And the third is the accessibility to a wide range of professionals who are willing to counsel the new generation of potential museum employees.

→ IDEAL CANDIDATE

Candidates must have a 3.0 GPA and must have completed the sophomore year of an undergraduate degree in an accredited academic program.

Candidates must be currently enrolled in an academic program at an accredited college or university.

Candidates must submit all required materials, including a completed application form (available on the PMA website: www.philamuseum. org/education/273-233.html), resume, official transcript, essay, and two letters of recommendation from faculty or other mentors.

→ APPLICATION PROCESS

Submission of application form, resume, transcript, essay and two letters of recommendation. High ranking applicants are interviewed in person or by phone. Final selections are made after the interviews.

Contact Information:

Address:
26th and Benjamin Franklin Parkway
Philadelphia, PA 19130

E-Mail Address:
jcooke@philamuseum.org

Phone Number:
215.684.7397

Website Address:
www.philamuseum.org/education/273-233.html

THE PROGRESSIVE GROUP OF INSURANCE COMPANIES

An integral part of our college graduate hiring program.

Industry:
Insurance

State(s) in Which Internships are Offered:
Colorado, Ohio

Monetary Compensation:
Yes

Compensation Structure for Internship Program:
IT interns:
Undergraduates: $14-20 per hour
Graduate: $18-24 per hour
Corporate Internships
(including Accounting, Actuarial, HR and Pricing Analysts):
Rising Seniors: $16-$18 per hour
Rising Juniors: $14-$16 per hour
Rising Sophomores: $13-$15 per hour

Intern Benefits:
• Complete housing assistance
• Partial relocation assistance
• Free parking
• Special events throughout the summer, including social activities and career-development events like "Lunch and Learns," which provide information about career opportunities and unique business initiatives like usage-based insurance.

Semesters that Internships are Offered:
Summer

Application Deadlines:
Generally March 30

→ **PROGRAM OVERVIEW**

In addition to the opportunity to develop your career and enjoy a summer in Cleveland or Colorado Springs, the opportunity to become a full-time Progressive person is one of the greatest incentives for students to accept an internship with us. Progressive offers great perks for all of its people, including one of the largest corporate art collections in the country, on-site fitness centers, and on-site health clinics. Full-time job offers are extended based on each intern's performance. Our goal is to find people who aren't afraid to risk, learn and grow.

→ **PROGRAM DESCRIPTION**

We seek highly motivated students who want to enhance their skills while working for a Fortune 500 company regarded for its innovation. We offer internships with our accounting, analytical, human resources, marketing, information technology, pricing and actuarial analysis, sales and service, and legal groups. We seek out people who display strong communication, customer service and leadership skills as well as the ability to be flexible and work in a fast-paced environment.

We plan a number of special events for our interns throughout the summer including social activities and career-development events like "Lunch and Learns," which provide information about career opportunities at Progressive as well as updates on business initiatives like our usage-based insurance product. This summer our interns attended a Cleveland Indians game, attended concerts, visited a local amusement park and learned how to network at a large company. Their calendar is packed with things to do and places to see in Cleveland and Colorado Springs. Being bored is not an option!

Our internships are paid positions – the average intern earned nearly $10,000 last summer – and in some cases housing is also provided.

→ PROGRAM UNIQUENESS

Progressive is an innovative company, and we look for people who are problem solvers, think fast on their feet, enjoy a challenge and take real pride in their work. Interns are assigned a project and given a deadline. From there, they have the freedom to shape their projects and their experience with us as they see fit. Interns become a part of the Progressive team and get a first-hand look at what it's like to be a full-time Progressive person. Interns obtain experience with hands-on projects. Each intern is assigned a manager and a mentor for his/her three-month internship.

→ IDEAL CANDIDATE

Prerequisites vary by position. For example, within IT, technical knowledge and skills are required. Candidates need to be currently enrolled in a bachelor's or master's program. Selection processes include a resume review, a phone or in-person interview with a Progressive recruiter, and in-person interviews with our hiring managers. Some positions require testing. All candidates are given a background check.

→ APPLICATION PROCESS

Applicants can apply online at: jobs.progressive.com by completing a profile and attaching their resume and cover letter. Students may also visit Progressive at college career events. Overall steps include: resume review; phone or in-person interview by a recruiter; and in-person interviews with two hiring managers. Some positions also require testing.

Contact Information:

Address:
6300 Wilson Mills Road
Mayfield Village, OH 44143

E-Mail Address:
laura_iwanycky@progressive.com

Phone Number:
800.321.9843

Website Address:
jobs.progressive.com

THE PUBLIC DEFENDER SERVICE FOR THE DISTRICT OF COLUMBIA

One of the pre-eminent legal internship opportunities available.

Industry:
Legal Services

State(s) in Which Internships are Offered:
District of Columbia

Monetary Compensation:
No

Compensation Structure for Internship Program:
N/A

Intern Benefits:
• On the job travel reimbursement
• Parking reimbursement
• Stipend and Fellowship availability
• Comprehensive training

Semesters that Internships are Offered:
Summer
Fall
Spring
Winter

Application Deadlines:
Winter Quarter - December 1st
Spring Semester - December 1st
Spring Quarter - February 1st
Summer Semester/Quarter - March 1st
Fall Semester/Quarter - August 1st

→ **PROGRAM OVERVIEW**

Rated one of the best internships in the country, the PDS Criminal Law Internship Program offers a hands-on investigative experience to undergraduate and graduate students. The program equips students with the fundamental investigative techniques and relevant criminal law knowledge required to provide exceptional investigative support to some of the best trial lawyers in the nation's capital. Hailed as "one of the finest pre-law experiences available" by the Washington Post and "a criminal law internship at its in-your-face best" by the Princeton Review, this program is for anyone looking for an adventurous semester outside of an office setting.

→ **PROGRAM DESCRIPTION**

The mission of the Public Defender Service (PDS) for the District of Columbia is to provide and promote quality legal representation to indigent adults and children facing a loss of liberty, and thereby protecting society's interest in the fair administration of justice. PDS's exceptional advocacy and proven success through individualized and continuous client representation has resulted in its designation as an exemplary defender office and a model for other jurisdictions.

The Intern Investigators participating in the Criminal Law Internship Program play a vital role in carrying out the PDS mission and contributing to its success. For all cases, a thorough investigation of the facts is a prerequisite for providing clients with the highest quality representation. Although PDS employs a staff of professional investigators, a significant portion of the investigative work is accomplished by the Intern Investigators. At the end of an intensive week-long training session, the Intern Investigators are assigned to work with attorneys in one of the legal services divisions. The attorneys work closely with their Intern Investigators, in a sense continuing the training process that began during the first week of the program. As the program progresses, additional

meetings and training sessions are scheduled to discuss topics that are relevant to the Intern Investigators' role.

Some of the responsibilities of an Intern Investigator include interviewing witnesses and clients, taking witness statements, performing criminal background checks, photographing and diagramming crime scenes, preparing courtroom exhibits, and writing investigative reports. Obviously, this is not a desk job. Nor is it simply an opportunity to observe an attorney at work. The Intern Investigators spend the majority of their time visiting local neighborhoods, local jails, police stations, and courthouses collecting information. Through their investigative efforts, Intern Investigators assist the attorneys in assessing the strengths and weaknesses of the charges brought against their clients. The information Intern Investigators uncover provides the building blocks necessary to support the case theory.

The PDS office environment is incredibly team-oriented. The PDS family is welcoming and supportive. Generally, casual attire is appropriate for Intern Investigators, unless they're needed to testify, when business attire is required. When in the office, Intern Investigators work in a lab where computer terminals and telephones are available. In addition to the comprehensive training opportunities, PDS also provides Intern Investigators with a tour and lecture series, court watching opportunities, and an LSAT discount through Kaplan and Princeton Review.

→ PROGRAM UNIQUENESS
A former PDS Intern Investigator said, "There is no greater challenge than to have someone relying on you to protect their freedom, and no greater satisfaction than when you meet that expectation." This program provides Intern Investigators with a once in a lifetime eye-opening opportunity that will stay with them for the rest of their lives, and a level of responsibility that is unmatched by other top programs. As another former Intern Investigator wrote, "I feel that my work at PDS had real meaning. I literally helped a man preserve his liberty."

→ IDEAL CANDIDATE
The program is open to undergraduates, recent graduates, and law students. All majors are welcome to apply. A full-time commitment and access to a vehicle is preferred, but not required. To be competitive, applicants must not only be able to express an understanding of our mission, but a commitment to our clients.

→ APPLICATION PROCESS
A complete application packet includes a resume, cover letter, program application, and essay response. Additional documentation is optional. Interviews with qualified applicants are conducted in person or over the phone. Interviews consist of both standard and hypothetical questions. Decisions are typically made within two weeks of the interview.

Contact Person: Chris Pipe

Address:
633 Indiana Ave., NW
Washington DC, 20004

E-Mail Address:
Internship@pdsdc.org

Phone Number:
202.824.2310

Website Address:
www.pdsdc.org

RESEARCH EXPERIENCES IN SOLID EARTH SCIENCE FOR STUDENTS (RESESS)

Summer research internship program in geophysics and geology for undergraduates.

Industry:
Not-For-Profit
State(s) in Which Internships are Offered:
All 50 states and the District of Columbia
Monetary Compensation:
Yes
Compensation Structure for Internship Program:
Interns work 40 hours a week and earn a competitive wage.
Intern Benefits: ●FREE●
• Complete housing assistance
• Complete relocation assistance
• Transportation stipend
• Meal allowance
• Free parking
• Round-trip airfare and furnished apartments are provided at no cost to interns
• Support to attend scientific conferences
Semesters that Internships are Offered:
Summer

Application Deadlines:
Students interested in applying for the RESESS program should submit an application before February 1 for the following summer.

→ PROGRAM OVERVIEW

Research Experiences in Solid Earth Science for Students (RESESS) is a paid, summer research internship program for undergraduate science, math, and engineering students interested in learning more about geophysics and geology. The main goal of RESESS is increasing diversity in the geosciences. Recruited after their sophomore or junior year in college, RESESS interns have structured mentoring, paid research internships, and a supported learning community.

RESESS is managed by UNAVCO in partnership with the United States Geological Survey and Incorporated Research Institutions for Seismology. The National Science Foundation is a major funding sponsor.

→ PROGRAM DESCRIPTION

The 10-week RESESS summer program typically starts in early June and continues through mid-August. RESESS interns work 40 hours a week participating in science research while earning a competitive wage. Round-trip airfare and furnished apartments are provided at no cost to interns.

RESESS provides up to 4 years of summer research experience; the first year's research is done with a scientist at University of Colorado Boulder or the United States Geological Survey in Golden, Colorado. Subsequent summers may be spent with researchers across the country. Throughout the program interns become part of a growing community of diverse young scientists. They are able to network with students and scientists around the world, develop skills in leadership and scientific writing, and collaborate with scientists on real research.

The program is designed to guide students to graduate school and beyond.

To view examples of interns' current and past research, visit www.resess.unavco.org.

→ PROGRAM UNIQUENESS

RESESS is dedicated to broadening participation in the solid earth sciences by encouraging the involvement of students from historically under-represented groups such as Black or African American, Hispanic or Latino, American Indian or Alaskan Native, and Native Hawaiian or other Pacific Islander.

→ IDEAL CANDIDATE

Students who will have completed their Sophomore or Junior year before the program begins and are enrolled in a science, math, or engineering program are eligible to apply to RESESS.

→ APPLICATION PROCESS

The completed application, including essay, two letters of recommendation and official transcript, are required. The application can be found online at www.resess.unavco.org.

Contact Person: Susan Eriksson
Address: 6350 Nautilus Drive Boulder, CO 80301
E-Mail Address: eriksson@unavco.org
Phone Number: 303.381.7466
Website Address: www.resess.unavco.org

RSM McGLADREY, INC. & McGLADREY & PULLEN LLP

An honest look at a career in public accounting.

Industry: Accounting	
State(s) in Which Internships are Offered: Arizona, California, Colorado, Connecticut, Florida, Illinois, Indiana, Iowa, Kansas, Maryland, Massachusetts, Minnesota, Missouri, Nebraska, Nevada, New Jersey, New York, North Carolina, Ohio, Pennsylvania, South Dakota, Texas, Virginia, Washington, Wisconsin	
Monetary Compensation: Yes	
Compensation Structure for Internship Program: Competitive, based on market conditions.	
Intern Benefits: • Sign on bonuses • Time and one-half for overtime	
Semesters that Internships are Offered: Summer, Winter	
Application Deadlines: Varies. Check with your school's Career Services function.	

→ PROGRAM OVERVIEW

McGladrey & Pullen LLP – a partner-owned CPA firm – delivers audit and attest services. RSM McGladrey provides financially-focused business services to mid-sized companies. Offering accounting, tax services, business consulting, retirement resources, employer services, corporate finance, wealth management and financial process outsourcing, RSM McGladrey Inc. serves clients' global business needs through its membership in RSM International (an affiliation of separate and independent accounting and consulting firms).

The alternative practice structure that exists between McGladrey & Pullen LLP and RSM McGladrey allows the two companies to work together in serving our clients' needs though separate and independent legal entities. Together, McGladrey & Pullen LLP and RSM McGladrey rank as the fifth-largest provider of accounting, tax and business consulting services, assisting clients from approximately 100 offices nationwide.

→ PROGRAM DESCRIPTION

While working with mid-sized, entrepreneurial businesses at McGladrey & Pullen, you will gain hands-on client experience and have direct contact with business owners. To further diversify your experiences, you will be involved with a variety of team engagements, allowing you to work on several pieces of any particular assignment – not just one small component.

Interns assist in providing quality CPA services to McGladrey & Pullen's clients by performing, in an efficient and effective manner, the duties and responsibilities listed below:

- Develop relationships with client employees.

- Become proficient in assisting clients with routine accounting functions.

- Become familiar with and adhere to McGladrey and Pullen's policies and procedures.

- Draft financial statements under prescribed format.

- Prepare portions of compilation, review and audit engagements.

- Have a working knowledge of all microcomputer applications routinely used.

- Have knowledge of accounting pronouncements and demonstrate a basic income tax understanding.

After joining McGladrey & Pullen, interns are assigned to mentors who will guide them through their early days and throughout their internship with us. Interns attend training programs and have the opportunity to work on diverse client engagements, including manufacturing, not-for-profit, government contracts, healthcare, construction and financial institution clients.

→ PROGRAM UNIQUENESS

Our interns gain valuable experience by working directly with mid-sized, entrepreneurial businesses – the most dynamic segment of the U.S. economy. The work given to them ensures a better understanding of the challenges our clients face and allows our interns to see first-hand the positive impact their work can have. Our interns and employees are exposed to key decision makers and company owners early in their career. This early exposure provides more responsibility, translating into challenging and rewarding careers.

Our internship experiences vary slightly from office to office, but most programs include:

Orientation and Training:
From their first week, interns are provided with the tools necessary to acclimate themselves to our organization. We provide both formal and on-the-job training to prepare interns for their roles and responsibilities.

Intern Program Events:
Our offices host formal and informal events throughout the internship period, from lunch-and-learn workshops to a night at a local sporting event or community service project.

Intern Webcast Series:
Our interns have the opportunity to attend periodic national webcasts hosted by firm leadership. These webcasts offer our interns insight into our leaders as individuals, their goals for the firm, and a perspective on our organization beyond the local market.

Performance Management:
Interns set goals during their time with the firm – these objectives are measured against those goals in determining opportunities for full-time employment with our firm.

Intern Capstone Event:
Our interns attend a 2 1/2 day national conference which focuses on defining and developing their career aspirations. This is an opportunity for interns to network with peers from across the country and to take some time to focus on their long-term development.

→ IDEAL CANDIDATE
Candidates must have a minimum B.A./B.S. degree in Accounting or equivalent from an accredited university and a minimum 3.0 GPA in the Accounting Major.

→ APPLICATION PROCESS
All must apply online at:
www.rsmmcgladrey.jobs

Contact Information:
Website Address:
http://www.rsmmcgladrey.com
or www.rsmmcgladrey.jobs

SCHNEIDER ASSOCIATES

SA internships are: Dynamic, Hands-On, Educational, Exciting, Fast-Paced, Creative...Limitless.

Industry: Communications/Media - Marketing/PR	
State(s) in Which Internships are Offered: Massachusetts	
Monetary Compensation: No	
Compensation Structure for Internship Program: N/A	
Intern Benefits: None	
Semesters that Internships are Offered: Summer, Fall, Spring, Winter	
Application Deadlines: N/A	

→ PROGRAM OVERVIEW

If you are interested in Public Relations, Marketing Communications, New Media, or Social Media and want to "learn by doing," Schneider Associates is a great place to grow your skills, gain valuable agency experience, build your portfolio and have fun.

→ PROGRAM DESCRIPTION

Schneider Associates explores strategies to successfully launch new products, services, companies and communities. A full-service public relations and marketing agency, Schneider Associates represents a wide range of consumer, corporate, real estate, and public affairs clients. We are located in the heart of Boston's Financial District and specialize in Launch Public Relations, a proprietary method of launching new products and revitalizing icon products to build and sustain awareness, excitement, and sales. Each semester, our interns participate in an SA Internship Orientation and an internship project surrounding LaunchPR, as well as industry and skill development workshops.

→ PROGRAM UNIQUENESS

We consider our interns an integral part of the account team and look for someone who is familiar with the communications field, a self-starter with an enthusiastic personality. We value opinions and encourage creativity.

→ IDEAL CANDIDATE

- Computer proficiency
- Superior writing ability
- Passion
- Ability to work 2-3 full days per week
- Web research skills
- A real interest in learning!

→ APPLICATION PROCESS

If you are interested in joining our team, please forward your resume and cover letter to internships@schneiderpr.com. If you have a blog, Twitter feed or LinkedIn profile, please send details. No phone calls.

Contact Information:	
Address: 2 Oliver Street, Suite 901 Boston, MA 02109	
E-Mail Address: internships@schneiderpr.com	
Phone Number: 617.536.3300	
Website Address: www.schneiderpr.com	

**THIS PAGE
INTENTIONALLY LEFT BLANK**

SIMS METAL MANAGEMENT

A challenging place to work - like nothing you've ever done!

Industry: Manufacturing	
State(s) in Which Internships are Offered: Connecticut, New Jersey, New York	
Monetary Compensation: Yes	
Compensation Structure for Internship Program: Based on skill set	
Intern Benefits: • Free parking • The opportunity to learn the scrap metal recycling business	
Semesters that Internships are Offered: Summer	
Application Deadlines: Varies annually	

→ PROGRAM OVERVIEW

We recruit talented people at the undergraduate level in the following degree programs:

❖ Electrical, Mechanical, Civil/Environmental Engineering

❖ Business Administration/Management

❖ Marketing and Communications

To be considered for our Internship Program, you must be in good academic standing and have exceptional leadership and communication skills. During the assignment, interns will learn our business processes, and will be mentored and given instruction that will help them apply academic theory to real-life issues. Interns will be exposed to a myriad of project-based assignments, allowing them to contribute to Sims while gaining immeasurable work experience.

→ PROGRAM DESCRIPTION

Sims Group is the world's leading metals and electronics recycling company, turning unwanted post-consumer items and industrial scrap into raw materials for manufacturing operations around the world. The North American Division maintains a network of equipment, processing facilities, transportation and communications operations. The recycling industry plays a crucial role in the protection of the environment by conserving natural resources and energy, supplying raw materials to manufacturing, and balancing the U.S. trade deficit.

At Sims, we realize that this all starts with our employees. We are constantly seeking talented individuals to intern in our organization as we develop our next generation of managers and leaders. Internships provide college students with a challenging work experience and an opportunity to expand their knowledge and understanding of work in a professional environment.

Sims Group accepts resumes year-round for selection into the Sims' Internship Program. We're looking for the brightest and the best people to help us run our business, and we welcome applications from all those who are appropriately qualified. We recruit talented people at the undergraduate level in several degree programs. Depending on your degree, background, and interests, you may qualify for one of our various placements that will compliment your academic studies. Opportunities are generally available in the following areas:

• Engineering (Electrical, Mechanical)
• Commercial/Trading
• Operations

- Environmental Health & Safety
- New Business Development
- Research

→ PROGRAM UNIQUENESS
The opportunity to work in the scrap metal industry.

→ IDEAL CANDIDATE
We recruit talented people at the undergraduate level in the following degree programs:

- Electrical
- Mechanical
- Civil/Environmental
- Engineering
- Business Administration/Management
- Marketing and Communications

→ APPLICATION PROCESS
Applicants first submit a resume and fill out a general application. Applicants will then be selected via three rounds of interviews.

Contact Information:

Address:
One Linden Avenue East
Jersey City, NJ 07305

E-Mail Address:
ALLISON.PETZKO@SIMSMM.COM

Phone Number:
201.577.3284

Website Address:
http://www.sims-group.com/us/hr/intern.asp

SITE SANTA FE

SITE offers a multifaceted experience working with cutting-edge contemporary art.

Industry:	
Arts & Entertainment	
State(s) in Which Internships are Offered:	
New Mexico	
Monetary Compensation:	
Yes	
Compensation Structure for Internship Program:	
N/A	
Intern Benefits:	
• College Credit	
• Stipend	
• Discount at museum book store	
Semesters that Internships are Offered:	
Winter/Spring, Summer, Fall	
Application Deadlines:	
Please see:	
www.sitesantafe.org for calendar deadlines	

→ PROGRAM OVERVIEW

Gain practical knowledge and have a meaningful experience as an intern at SITE Santa Fe! SITE's Internship Program introduces participants to the operations of an internationally renowned contemporary art venue. Interns become familiar with the spectrum of daily activities with a "behind the scenes" perspective, while gaining a broader understanding of the institution. SITE Santa Fe values its interns for their fresh ideas and high level of energy.

→ PROGRAM DESCRIPTION

An intern can select the department in which to intern. Below is a job description for each department:

Exhibitions and Operations:
SITE Santa Fe provides year-round exhibitions of cutting-edge contemporary art with regional, national, and international significance. Envisioned as an art exhibition space similar to the European *kunsthalle*, SITE originates and organizes exhibitions and is a major venue for national and international traveling exhibitions. An internship with the Exhibitions and Operations department would involve working directly with the Director of Operations, the Operations Manager, the Thaw Curatorial Fellow, preparators, curators, and artists. Areas of emphasis would include operation of the facility, exhibition maintenance, registrarial duties, installation of exhibitions, assistance with planning for upcoming exhibitions, packing and shipping of artworks, researching artists, exhibits and other art institutions, and maintaining exhibition archives.

Education and Public Programs:
The goal of SITE Santa Fe's Education and Public Programs department is to make contemporary art accessible to a wide range of audiences. In order to bring greater understanding of our exhibitions of contemporary art to adults and young people, SITE presents a broad scope of public programs. These include lectures, panel discussions, dialogues, and performances with well-known artists, poets, and musicians.

Education programs include exhibition tours with SITE Guides, outreach workshops in the public schools, and collaborations with youth-oriented service organizations. An intern working with the Education and Public Programs department will obtain hands-on experience in working directly with a wide variety of groups. Additionally, the intern will assist in the facilitation of education and outreach programs.

Development and Public Relations/Marketing:

The Development and PR/Marketing department focuses its energies on fundraising, marketing, and promotion. This five-member team is responsible for raising nearly $2 million annually through museum memberships, individual donations, foundation and corporate giving, and benefit events. We employ a variety of marketing and promotional tools to ensure international, national, and local visibility for SITE Santa Fe including the management of an organizational website, media outreach, and the design, production and distribution of print materials. An intern working with the Development and PR/Marketing department will provide critical support on a variety of special events, fundraising, and promotional projects, giving the intern in-depth knowledge and experience in this important area of non-profit arts management.

→ PROGRAM UNIQUENESS

Department heads, educators, and administrators help interns gain a broader understanding of SITE Santa Fe's structure and exhibitions as well as insight into the greater international art world. Meetings with departments are arranged to familiarize interns with the spectrum of daily activities behind the scenes at our institution. SITE Santa Fe encourages interns to consider practical and theoretical questions about the art community.

→ IDEAL CANDIDATE

Anyone may apply. We are looking for those who will be a good fit with SITE Santa Fe. Internship positions are based on museum needs and requirements along with applicant's skills and interests.

→ APPLICATION PROCESS

Applicants must fill out a form that includes resume information as well as responses to questions about contemporary art. One letter of recommendation is required.

The application is downloadable from: www.sitesantafe.org

Selected applicants will interview with the intern supervisor and department head.

Contact Person: Joanne Lefrak

Address:
1606 Paseo de Peralta
Santa Fe, NM 87501

E-Mail Address:
lefrak@sitesantafe.org

Phone Number:
505.989.1199

Website Address:
www.sitesantafe.org

SOUTHWEST AIRLINES

Interns say: "unforgettable", "motivating", "unrivaled", "treasured", "FUN", "thrilling", "family", "rich".

Industry: Transportation	
State(s) in Which Internships are Offered: Arizona, California, Illinois, Maryland, Texas	
Monetary Compensation: Yes	
Compensation Structure for Internship Program: Between $8 and $20 an hour depending on the particular internship and requirements.	
Intern Benefits: • Free parking • Free flight benefits on Southwest • Casual dress: shorts and t-shirts • Training and development classes • Many FUN Southwest Culture events	•FREE•
Semesters that Internships are Offered: Summer, Fall, Spring	
Application Deadlines: **Summer:** October through November of previous year **Fall:** February through March of current year **Spring:** August through September of previous year	

→ PROGRAM OVERVIEW

Intern with me and fly for free... All Southwest Airlines Interns are able to fly free on Southwest and believe me, they take advantage of it! Ever want to fly to another city just for dinner, go home on the weekend for some of Mom's cooking, or go on a 24 hour adventure to Vegas? Southwest Interns can do all that without spending a dime on airfare. You work, too—meaningful, important work for Southwest Airlines. You are treated and valued like an employee and part of the Southwest Airlines Team.

→ PROGRAM DESCRIPTION

Southwest continues to rank as the largest U.S., carrier in terms of passengers carried, according to the most recent figures released by the U.S. Department of Transportation's Bureau of Transportation Statistics. Among all industries in 2007, Fortune Magazine listed Southwest Airlines as number five among America's Top Ten most admired corporations.

The "NoLimits" Internship Program gives students quality, real-world experience, an insider's glance into this fascinating industry, and is guaranteed to be a FUN semester! The goal of the "NoLimits" Internship is to provide Interns with interactive learning opportunities and hands-on business experience. Each Intern will be exposed to practical workplace skills needed for his/her business field. The Intern will be able to validate his/her career decisions through this opportunity to apply classroom knowledge.

Internship opportunities include, but are not limited to:

- Advertising
- Charitable Giving
- Community Relations
- Corporate Tax
- Dispatch
- Executive Office (various positions)
- Facilities
- Finance (various positions)
- Flight Operations
- Flight Operations – Publications
- Graphic Design & Creative Services
- Ground Operations (various positions)
- InFlight

- Internal Audit
- Legislative Communications & Grassroots
- Maintenance (various positions)
- Marketing (various positions)
- Meteorology
- Operational Safety
- People
- Promotions
- Public Relations
- Purchasing
- Revenue Management
- Schedule Planning
- Safety and Environmental
- Strategic Planning and Implementation
- Technology

Interns participate in FUN activities just for them like Happy Hour, Amazing Race, & Water Wars. They can also share in our unique culture with events such as Deck Parties, Halloween, Chili Cook-Off, Message to the Field, and Boeing Burgers & Beer Bash.

Some of our Interns land jobs at SWA upon graduation. To help that, they are able to participate in Career Day where they get interviewing tips, resume help, and a chance to learn about other departments within Southwest. In addition to that, Interns are encouraged to spend "days in the field" with departments in which they have additional interest.

→ PROGRAM UNIQUENESS
Southwest's Interns say it best:

❖ *"Being treated as F-A-M-I-L-Y."*

❖ *"Working with People that actually LUV their jobs."*

❖ *"Engaging in a unique Corporate Culture. Where else can Interns play basketball with a Vice President?"*

❖ *"Gaining insight into the aviation world while having FUN!!!"*

❖ *"Traveling, inside operations meetings, and tasting all the flavors of the multi-faceted industry, NoLimits is more than just work experience."*

❖ *"Interns are immediately a part of the Southwest LUV."*

❖ *"Southwest's amazing Company Culture!"*

❖ *"Contributing to a successful business. Doing real work, learning the same things as fulltime Employees, and working with Leaders."*

→ IDEAL CANDIDATE
Each position is different; complete job descriptions with requirements can be found on our website. All applicants must be full-time students and have authorization to work in the United States. Most are for Junior and Senior level students, but some allow Sophomores. We are looking for candidates with a Warrior Spirit, a Servant's Heart, and a Fun-LUVing Attitude.

→ APPLICATION PROCESS
Candidates apply on our website, answer qualifying questions, and attach a resume. After the deadline, the process takes 4-8 weeks for resume review, phone screens, and interviews. Candidates may be requested to submit an essay, transcript, and letters of reference. All candidates are contacted after decisions are made.

Contact Person: Greg Muccio

Address:
2702 Love Field Drive, HDQ 4HR
Dallas, TX 75235

E-Mail Address:
nolimits@wnco.com

Phone Number:
214.792.4457

Website Address:
http://www.southwest.com/careers/internships.html

SOUTHWESTERN COMPANY

Developing Entrepreneurs
Since 1868.

Industry: Communications/Media - Publishing/Print Media	
State(s) in Which Internships are Offered: All 50 states (except Hawaii) and the District of Columbia	
Monetary Compensation: No	
Compensation Structure for Internship Program: N/A	
Intern Benefits: None	
Semesters that Internships are Offered: Summer	
Application Deadlines: No specific deadlines	

→ PROGRAM OVERVIEW

Southwestern is one of America's most successful private companies, built by, led by, and owned primarily by graduates of our summer internship program. After you successfully complete the internship program, with the recommendation of your manager, you will have a choice of careers in fields such as sales, sales management, accounting, finance, or marketing in one of our diverse companies. Or, you may qualify to build your own company using the capital, support and resources of our business incubator.

→ PROGRAM DESCRIPTION

Southwestern is a summer work internship for college students that gives them:

- Unmatched experience for a powerful resume

- Extraordinary financial opportunity

- Life skills training

- Challenge

- Mentoring from the best

- A stepping-stone to their goals in life, whatever they may be.

Southwestern is the gateway into an amazing career in one of our 15 companies, or into the resources, experience, and mindset to partner with you in building a new company.

Some of the benefits our company offers are personal growth, increased communication and life skills, resume-building, the opportunity to travel, and, of course, a real challenge.

But employment with us is not for everybody. Some of the challenges you may face are long hours, time spent away from home, no absolute guarantees for the future, separation from school friends, no floor or ceiling for earnings and, let's face it— it's not exactly glamorous.

→ PROGRAM UNIQUENESS

In the Southwestern Program, students have an opportunity to run their own business, marketing educational books and software to families in their homes.

Southwestern has helped well over 100,000 students finance their college education while picking up marketable skills along the way.

→ IDEAL CANDIDATE

Any student who has completed their first year in their college or university in any major is eligible to apply.

→ APPLICATION PROCESS

Apply at www.southwestern.com or call 1.880.843.6149.

Contact Person: Trey Campbell

Address:
2451 Atrium Way
Nashville, TN 37214

E-Mail Address:
trey.campbell@southwestern.com

Phone Number:
800.843.6149

Website Address:
www.southwestern.com

T. ROWE PRICE

Working and learning in a progressive environment with talented professionals.

Industry:
Finance/Banking -
Financial Services/Planning

State(s) in Which
Internships are Offered:
All primary T. Rowe Price locations.

Monetary Compensation:
Yes

Compensation Structure for Internship Program:
Competitive, based on market conditions.

Intern Benefits:
• Partial housing assistance
• Partial relocation assistance
• Partial fitness center membership

Semesters that
Internships are Offered:
Summer

Application Deadlines:
Varies.
Please check individual job postings.

→ PROGRAM OVERVIEW

Experience what's to come after graduation as a summer intern at T. Rowe Price, a leading global investment management firm based in Baltimore, Maryland. A summer internship with T. Rowe Price offers a meaningful experience that will help position your future career for success. You will become part of a thriving business environment where you can apply your academic knowledge and grow, both personally and professionally. With ongoing guidance and coaching from your manager and coworkers, you will work on real-world projects that contribute to our success as a global investment management firm.

→ PROGRAM DESCRIPTION

To continue to grow and remain competitive, T. Rowe Price must continually attract and retain high-caliber talent. Our internship program is one way to achieve this goal. We seek to hire successful interns for subsequent summers and develop them into promising candidates for rewarding, full-time careers with T. Rowe Price. Along with offering a meaningful work experience through your projects, our program is designed to enhance your internship experience by exposing you to our organization and culture.

This is achieved by offering you the following:

❖ Foundations for Interns, a one-day orientation program introducing you to T. Rowe Price's mission, values, company history, and culture.

❖ Networking events with managers, associates, and other interns throughout the firm. These events provide the avenue for you to build valuable business relationships.

❖ Leadership speaker series with T. Rowe Price senior management - This series is conducted monthly and provides a forum for interns to attend several business presentations offered by senior leaders. During these one-hour lunch sessions, senior leaders will present on various topics of interest including company culture, the investment management industry, and significant T. Rowe Price initiatives.

❖ Learning and skill enhancement through professional development activities - You will be invited to attend several workshops during your internship. Prior workshops for first-year interns include Working with Behavioral Styles and Presentation Skills. Returning interns have also attended our Investment School and Career Success Skills workshops.

❖ Community outreach opportunities will be available to you through our company Days of Caring. By participating in these one-day volunteer activities, you will be part of the valuable role T. Rowe Price plays in the community.

❖ Objective setting and performance evaluation - Clear objectives will be established between you and your manager at the beginning of your internship. At the end of your internship, your manager will meet with you to evaluate the results of your work against your objectives and discuss your strengths and developmental areas along with opportunities for successive internships or regular employment upon graduation.

❖ End of internship presentation - You will be required to conduct a 15-minute formal presentation to managers and other business associates at the conclusion of your internship. This presentation provides an opportunity to showcase your work experience and gain exposure to various managers throughout the organization.

→ PROGRAM UNIQUENESS

T. Rowe Price offers a well-structured intern program designed to attract and retain high-quality, talented interns who ultimately convert to regular associates. The company provides a collaborative culture where interns gain valuable work experience, establish business relationships, and add value to our organization.

→ IDEAL CANDIDATE

Program requirements include:

Undergraduate:
Full-time student entering sophomore, junior, or senior year of study.

Major: Related to internship position.

Minimum GPA:
3.0 overall; please see job postings for other specific requirements.

→ APPLICATION PROCESS

Apply direct online at:
www.troweprice.com/careers
or contact your career services office.

Contact Information

Website Address:
www.troweprice.com/careers

TRELLEBORG SEALING SOLUTIONS

Unique experience with global corporation.

Industry: Manufacturing	
State(s) in Which Internships are Offered:  California, Colorado, Illinois, Indiana, Oregon, Pennsylvania, South Carolina, Texas	
Monetary Compensation: 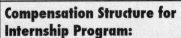 No	
Compensation Structure for Internship Program: N/A	
Intern Benefits: None	
Semesters that Internships are Offered: Summer, Fall, Spring, Winter	
Application Deadlines: No deadlines	

Our locations in the United States include: Portland, Oregon; Fresno, California; Torrance, California; Houston, Texas; Broomfield, Colorado; Lombard, Illinois; Fort Wayne, Indiana; North Charleston, South Carolina; and Conshohocken, Pennsylvania

→ PROGRAM UNIQUENESS
We are a global seal manufacturer and internships offer work experience and interaction with employees and customers in the Americas, Europe and Asia

→ IDEAL CANDIDATE
College student

→ APPLICATION PROCESS
College students work through their universities' intern programs.

→ PROGRAM OVERVIEW
Internships through local universities

→ PROGRAM DESCRIPTION
Internships with Trelleborg Sealing Solutions are offered through local universities. We typically partner with the universities that offer Co-op Programs in Engineering, Communications, Human Resources, Finance, and Research & Development.

Contact Person: Lori Replin

Address:
2531 Bremer Road
Fort Wayne, IN 46803

E-Mail Address:
lori.replin@trelleborg.com

Phone Number:
260.749.9631

Website Address:
www.tss.trelleborg.com/us

**THIS PAGE
INTENTIONALLY LEFT BLANK**

TURNER CONSTRUCTION COMPANY

Building Relationships *
Influencing Change * Developing
Goals * Experiencing Turner

Industry:
General Contractor

**State(s) in Which
Internships are Offered:**
Alabama, Arizona, California, Colorado,
Connecticut, District of Columbia, Florida,
Georgia, Illinois, Indiana, Kansas, Maryland,
Massachusetts, Michigan, Nevada,
New Jersey, New York, North Carolina, Ohio,
Oregon, Pennsylvania, South Carolina,
Tennessee, Texas, Virginia, Washington

Monetary Compensation:
Yes

**Compensation Structure for
Internship Program:**
Turner offers a competitive hourly
compensation rate customized to each
intern based on a number of factors such as
college school year, prior internship
experience, and location.

Intern Benefits:
• Housing assistance is provided
in some of our locations
• Interns receive year of service accrual
which counts toward service-related
benefits
• We offer feedback and performance
evaluations for every intern at the end
of the internship

**Semesters that
Internships are Offered:**
Summer

Application Deadlines:
Internship application deadlines
vary by office, but students should
plan to apply between January and March
for summer opportunities.

→ PROGRAM OVERVIEW
Turner provides internship and co-op experience to students through its personalized BRIDGE program. The Turner BRIDGE program is one of the industry's most comprehensive and competitive internship experiences for undergraduates seeking a career in construction. The BRIDGE program is more than a summer job — it's a professional and educational process that prepares students for a successful transition to a challenging and rewarding career.

→ PROGRAM DESCRIPTION
As a leader in our industry, Turner Construction places high value on internship experience when making hiring decisions. Through our own internship and co-op program, we strive to shape the future leaders of our company. As a Turner intern, you'll be challenged to realize your own potential. You'll learn from Turner professionals and immerse yourself in real project work. From day one, you're an important member of our team.

The BRIDGE program is a structured series of events designed to provide you with a well-rounded view of life at Turner.

The typical sequence includes:

• Participating in new hire orientation.
• Setting goals for learning and development.
• Receiving guidance from Turner mentors.
• Working on actual client projects and visiting job sites.
• Interacting with other interns on specials projects.

- Attending educational sessions with Turner executives and other speakers.
- Enjoying social and professional networking events.
- Receiving feedback and a formal evaluation from immediate supervisor.

→ PROGRAM UNIQUENESS

Turner provides students an invaluable, meaningful work experience, a sense of contribution to the community, hopefully some new friends and, most importantly, the feeling of being valued. Unlike many programs, prior Turner interns are given strong consideration for full-time employment after graduation. Turner is also recognized as a great place to work in rankings by Universum, The Black Collegian, Building Design and Construction Magazine, CollegeGrad.com, and others. So why not intern with a well-known visionary and pioneer in the construction industry?

→ IDEAL CANDIDATE

Our ideal internship candidates are:

- Freshmen, Sophomores, or Juniors currently enrolled at a four-year institution.

- Majoring in Engineering, Construction Management, Safety, or Architectural Studies.

- Proactive, open-minded, eager to learn, and willing to work hard as part of a team.

→ APPLICATION PROCESS

After submitting an application, we contact you to set up a visit to our office. The selection process typically consists of a number of interviews so that both Turner and the student have the opportunity to determine if it's a good match. Once an offer is extended, we work closely with you to determine a start date and project assignment.

Contact Information:

Address:
375 Hudson Street
New York, NY 10014

E-Mail Address:
corprecruiting@tcco.com

Phone Number:
212.229.6000

Website Address:
www.turnerconstruction.com

UNILEVER

Engaging projects with tangible results.

Industry:	
Consumer Products	

State(s) in Which Internships are Offered:
Arkansas, California, Connecticut, Georgia, Illinois, Indiana, Kansas, Kentucky, Maryland, Minnesota, New Jersey, North Carolina, Ohio, Pennsylvania, Rhode Island, Tennessee, Texas, Virginia, Washington

Monetary Compensation:
Yes

Compensation Structure for Internship Program:
Average intern hourly wage: $17.07

Intern Benefits:
- Complete housing assistance
- Transportation stipend
- Free parking
- Summer Hours Program Access to company store (varies by location)

Semesters that Internships are Offered:
Summer, Fall, Spring

Application Deadlines:
None

→ PROGRAM OVERVIEW

Could you work with some of the world's biggest, most popular brands? Unilever is looking for resourceful individuals with a will and the skills to succeed! In return, Unilever will give you the tools and opportunity so that together you can make Unilever brands more popular than ever before. You may not realize it, but you probably have a Unilever brand in your home. Look in your kitchen and bathroom shelves... you'll see Unilever brands there!

→ PROGRAM DESCRIPTION

Unilever's mission is to add vitality to life. We meet everyday needs for nutrition, hygiene, and personal care with brands that help people feel good, look good, and get more out of life. Each day, around the world, consumers make 160 million decisions to purchase Unilever products. In the United States, the portfolio includes major brand icons such as: Axe, Ben & Jerry's, Bertolli, Breyers, Caress, Country Crock, Degree, Dove personal care products, Hellmann's, Klondike, Knorr, Lipton, Popsicle, Promise, Q-Tips, Skippy, Slim-Fast, Suave, Sunsilk and Vaseline. All of the preceding brand names are registered trademarks of the Unilever Group of Companies.

The purpose of the Unilever Summer Internship Program is to introduce students to Unilever through a challenging and rewarding experience that offers them the opportunity to contribute to critical business goals. BusinessWeek has ranked Unilever among the Top 50 companies with best internships! Unilever has summer internships in Marketing, Finance, IT, Customer Development (Sales), and R&D. Unilever also has 6-month co-op internships in their Supply Chain and R&D functions.

Unilever's internship program can be a fast track to full-time employment at Unilever. Unilever's program is structured around an individual project that is developed with two objectives: 1) providing exposure to the business in a real and tangible way for the Intern and 2) gaining insights and results from a fresh and innovative perspective. On the first day of the internship, interns are given an orientation about Unilever, and what to expect during the internship. Interns will be exposed to group work, and in many areas, interns will be working cross-functionally. At the end of the internship, the intern project is presented to leaders of the business.

Many Unilever employees will say that one of the reasons they chose Unilever was because of the corporate culture. Employees are encouraged to come up with new ideas and fresh ways of doing things, while achieving outstanding results. In addition, Unilever understands the importance of diversity and that's why it is a critical component of its business strategy and an integral part of everything they value and do. Unilever is dedicated to being a good corporate citizen and neighbor. During the internship, interns will get the opportunity to take part in community service through Unilever's partnerships with organizations by making vital contributions that help improve daily living and strengthen local communities. Unilever's long history of strong values, responsible behavior, and a clear commitment to corporate social responsibility is an integral part of its operating tradition.

→ PROGRAM UNIQUENESS

Unilever is the world's 3rd largest CPG, and the experience you will get at Unilever is invaluable. Great brands come from understanding and connecting with consumers. Unilever is always developing new products, improving its brands, and promoting better, more efficient ways of working with their markets. You are a Unilever consumer, and your work will add value to its business! Unilever is home to some of the most innovative and inspiring people in the industry. Unilever employees learn from the best! During the internship, you will have an intense desire to impact the marketplace too, and thrive in Unilever's dynamic and exciting environment.

CANDIDATES MUST BE LEGALLY AUTHORIZED TO WORK IN THE UNITED STATES

→ IDEAL CANDIDATE
Marketing and Finance:
1st year MBA's and Juniors

Customer Development:
Sophomores and Juniors

IT:
Sophomores and Juniors

R&D:
Sophomores, Juniors, Seniors, and PhD's

Supply Chain:
Sophomores, Juniors, and Seniors

→ APPLICATION PROCESS

Students will need to build their profile and submit their resume online at www.unileverusa-graduates.com. Unilever will conduct one round of on-campus interviews at designated schools as well as phone screens with candidates who apply to the posting online. After an interview, students will receive an interview status within several days.

Contact Information

Address:
800 Sylvan Avenue
Englewood Cliffs, NJ 07632

E-Mail Address:
www.unileverusa-graduates.com

Website Address:
www.unileverusa-graduates.com

WOLF TECHNICAL

Complex problem solving with unique and challenging work.

Industry: Defense	
State(s) in Which Internships are Offered: Indiana	
Monetary Compensation: Yes	
Compensation Structure for Internship Program: $15-$25 per hour, 40 hour work week	
Intern Benefits: • Free parking • The benefit of doing real engineering work in a demanding Department of Defense research and development setting.	FREE
Semesters that Internships are Offered: Summer	
Application Deadlines: May 1st	

→ PROGRAM OVERVIEW
Interns at Wolf work closely with established engineers to create solutions that improve safety for military personnel. Also, the interns at Wolf work with our Forensic engineers in support of our legal support work.

→ PROGRAM DESCRIPTION
Our interns work in a hands-on environment doing real engineering and development work that positively affects the lives of others. We are committed to scientific truths and expect the same from our interns. During their time with Wolf, interns have helped improve safety for military personnel with several applications to date.

→ PROGRAM UNIQUENESS
Our workers are hands-on with responsibilities to project teams as well as to our clients from around the U.S. When they leave Wolf, they have worked on very important technical challenges and have supported our valued clients.

→ IDEAL CANDIDATE
Engineering course of study in several disciplines.

→ APPLICATION PROCESS
Forward a resume, schedule a personal interview, screening by 2-3 Wolf personnel, offer.

Contact Information:

E-Mail Address:
jward@wolftechnical.com

Website Address:
www.wolftechnical.com

**THIS PAGE
INTENTIONALLY LEFT BLANK**

WORLDTEACH

Contribute to international education as volunteer teachers in developing countries.

Industry:
Not-For-Profit

State and Countries in Which Internships are Offered:
Massachusetts, American Samoa, Bangladesh, Bulgaria, Chile, China, Colombia, Costa Rica, Ecuador, Guyana, Kenya, Marshall Islands, Micronesia, Namibia, Poland, Rwanda, South Africa and Thailand

Monetary Compensation:
Yes

Compensation Structure for Internship Program:
Interns receive a monthly stipend designed to cover their day-to-day living expenses based on the local cost of living.

Intern Benefits:
- Complete housing assistance
- Complete relocation assistance
- Transportation stipend
- Meal allowance
- Health insurance
- Our interns also receive the full-time support of in-country field staff and participate in Orientation which provides language and teaching instruction as well as cultural adjustment seminars.

Semesters that Internships are Offered:
Summer, Fall, Spring, Winter

Application Deadlines:
As WorldTeach programs depart throughout the year, application deadlines vary.
Please see:
www.worldteach.org/apply/deadlines.html

→ PROGRAM OVERVIEW

WorldTeach is a non-profit, non-governmental organization that helps individuals make a meaningful contribution to international education by working as volunteer teachers in developing countries. WorldTeach offers summer, semester or year-long programs to American Samoa, Bangladesh, Bulgaria, Chile, China, Colombia, Costa Rica, Ecuador, Guyana, Kenya, Marshall Islands, Micronesia, Namibia, Poland, Rwanda, South Africa and Thailand. Volunteers are placed in disadvantaged communities to teach English and, depending on the program, subjects such as math, science, computer studies and HIV/AIDS education, at the primary, secondary or university level. Volunteers receive training, language preparation, and field support, empowering them to make a lasting impact.

→ PROGRAM DESCRIPTION

WorldTeach was founded by a group of Harvard students in 1986, in response to the need for educational assistance in developing countries. It also addressed a growing interest among people in the U.S. and elsewhere to serve, teach and learn as volunteers overseas. Since its inception, WorldTeach has placed thousands of volunteer educators in communities throughout Asia, Latin America, Africa, Eastern Europe and the Pacific.

Based at the Center for International Development at Harvard University, WorldTeach offers the benefits of a well-established volunteer organization, while also providing more comprehensive, personalized support as a small NGO. Program fees cover round-trip international airfare, supplemental overseas medical coverage, three to four week Orientation training, site placements, 24-hour field support and networking opportunities. WorldTeach Volunteers work as full-time teachers, as employees of their host school or sponsoring institution in their placement country. Most volunteers live with a host family or on the school campus, and participate fully in the life of their host community.

The field staff visits placement sites to ensure that teaching and living arrangements are suitable. Along with room and board, Volunteers receive a monthly stipend for the duration of their program.

Each long-term WorldTeach program begins with a 3-4 week in-country orientation. This intense training period includes cross-cultural adjustment seminars, teacher training, health and safety tips, and language lessons. Summer programs begin with an intensive one-week orientation. WorldTeach volunteers come from diverse backgrounds throughout the U.S. and abroad. Volunteers can be recent college graduates, current college students (for summer programs), working professionals, married couples, retirees, or anyone else committed to international service and education. While no teaching or foreign language experience is required, volunteers should be flexible and ready to deal with the often unpredictable nature of living and working in a developing country. For more information about WorldTeach and the programs we offer, please visit our website at: www.worldteach.org or email us at: info@worldteach.org.

→ PROGRAM UNIQUENESS
Through a WorldTeach placement, volunteer teachers help students learn English, which is increasingly important for access to jobs, higher education, and the international community. Volunteers also build lasting friendships, experience the local culture and contribute to the activities and development of their host community. They gain cultural understanding and the ability to work independently in a new environment while also developing skills, including teaching, language, cross-cultural communication, and leadership abilities. WorldTeach is an opportunity that will stay with them for life and enhance their potential in many career fields.

→ IDEAL CANDIDATE
WorldTeach volunteers must be native English speakers at least 18 years old. For our semester and year-long programs, volunteers must also have a Bachelor's degree. Applicants should have an interest in teaching and international development as well as a commitment to community service

→ APPLICATION PROCESS
Part I of the WorldTeach application is submitted online at: www.worldteach.org/apply. Part II of the application includes three essays, a resume in WorldTeach format, two references (either professional or academic) a college/university transcript (semester and year-long programs only) and an interview with a returned volunteer (semester and year-long programs only).

Contact Information

Address:
Center for International Development
Harvard University
79 John F. Kennedy Street
Box 122
Cambridge, MA 02138

E-Mail Address:
info@worldteach.org

Phone Number:
617.495.5527

Website Address:
www.worldteach.org